MYTH AND REALITY

Myth
Mythology

MYTH AND REALITY

MIRCEA ELIADE

*Translated from the French
by Willard R. Trask*

HARPER TORCHBOOKS
Harper & Row, Publishers, New York
Grand Rapids, Philadelphia, St. Louis, San Francisco
London, Singapore, Sydney, Tokyo, Toronto

First HARPER PAPERBACK edition published 1975.

Library of Congress Catalog Card Number: 63-16508.

ISBN: 0-06-131369-6

90 26 25 24

Contents

I.

The Structure of Myths

FOR THE past fifty years at least, Western scholars have approached the study of myth from a viewpoint markedly different from, let us say, that of the nineteenth century. Unlike their predecessors, who treated myth in the usual meaning of the word, that is, as "fable," "invention," "fiction," they have accepted it as it was understood in the archaic societies, where, on the contrary, "myth" means a "true story" and, beyond that, a story that is a most precious possession because it is sacred, exemplary, significant. This new semantic value given the term "myth" makes its use in contemporary parlance somewhat equivocal. Today, that is, the word is employed both in the sense of "fiction" or "illusion" and in that familiar especially to ethnologists, sociologists, and historians of religions, the sense of "sacred tradition, primordial revelation, exemplary model."

The history of the different meanings given to the word "myth" in the antique and Christian worlds will be treated later (cf. Chaps. VIII and IX). Everyone knows that from the time of Xenophanes (*ca.* 565–470)—who was the first to criticize and reject the "mythological" expressions of the divinity employed by Homer and Hesiod—the Greeks steadily continued to empty *mythos* of all religious and metaphysical value. Contrasted both with *logos* and, later, with *historia, mythos* came in the end to denote "what cannot really exist." On its side, Judaeo-Christianity put the stamp of "falsehood" and "illusion" on whatever was not justified or validated by the two Testaments.

It is not in this sense—the most usual one in contemporary parlance—that we understand "myth." More precisely, it is not the intellectual stage or the historical moment when myth became a "fiction" that interests us. Our study will deal primarily with those societies in which myth is—or was until very recently—"living," in the sense that it supplies models for human behavior and, by that very fact, gives meaning and value to life. To understand the structure and function of myths in these traditional societies not only serves to clarify a stage in the history of human thought but also helps us to understand a category of our contemporaries.

To give only one example—that of the "cargo cults" of Oceania—it would be difficult to interpret this whole series of isolated activities without reference to their justification by myths. These prophetic and millennialist cults announce the imminence of a fabulous age of plenty and happiness. The natives will again be the masters in their islands, and they will no longer work, for the dead will return in magnificent ships laden with goods like the giant cargoes that the whites receive in their ports. It is for this reason that most of the "cargo cults" demand that, while all domestic animals and tools are to be destroyed, huge warehouses are to be built in which to store the goods brought by the dead. One movement prophesies Christ's arrival on a loaded freighter; another looks for the coming of "America." A new paradisal era will begin and the members of the cult will become immortal. Some cults also involve orgiastic acts, for the taboos and customs sanctioned by tradition will lose their reason for existence and give place to absolute freedom. Now, all these actions and beliefs are explained by *the myth of the destruction of the World, followed by a new Creation and the establishment of the Golden Age.* (We shall return to this myth later.)

Similar phenomena occurred in the Congo when the country became independent in 1960. In some villages the inhabitants tore the roofs off their huts to give passage to the gold coins that their ancestors were to rain down. Elsewhere everything was allowed to go to rack and ruin except the roads to the cemetery, by which the ancestors would make their way to the village. Even the orgiastic excesses had a meaning, for, according to the myth, from the dawn of the New Age all women would belong to all men.

In all probability phenomena of this kind will become more and more uncommon. We may suppose that "mythical behavior" will disappear as a result of the former colonies' acquiring political independence. But what is to happen in a more or less distant future will not help us to understand what has just happened. What we most need is to grasp the meaning of these strange forms of behavior, to understand the cause and the justification for these excesses. For to understand them is to see them as human phenomena, phenomena of culture, creations of the human spirit, not as a pathological outbreak of instinctual behavior, bestiality, or sheer childishness. There is no other alternative. Either we do our utmost to deny, minimize, or forget these excesses, taking them as isolated examples of "savagery" that will vanish completely as soon as the tribes have been "civilized," or we make the necessary effort to understand the mythical antecedents that explain and justify such excesses and give them a religious value. This latter approach is, we feel, the only one that even deserves consideration. It is only from a historico-religious viewpoint that these and similar forms of behavior can be seen as what they are—cultural phenomena—and lose their character of aberrant childishness or instinct run wild.

Value of "primitive mythologies"

All the great Mediterranean and Asiatic religions have mythologies. But it is better not to begin the study of myth from the starting point of, say, Greek or Egyptian or Indian mythology. Most of the Greek myths were recounted, and hence modified, adjusted, systematized, by Hesiod and Homer, by the rhapsodes and the mythographers. The mythological traditions of the Near East and of India have been sedulously reinterpreted and elaborated by their theologians and ritual-ists. This is not to say, of course, that (1) these Great My-thologies have lost their "mythical substance" and are only "literatures" or that (2) the mythological traditions of archaic societies were not rehandled by priests and bards. Just like the Great Mythologies that were finally transmitted as written texts, the "primitive" mythologies, discovered by the earliest travelers, missionaries, and ethnographers in the "oral" stage, have a "history." In other words, they have been transformed and enriched in the course of the ages under the influence of higher cultures or through the creative genius of exception-ally gifted individuals.

Nevertheless, it is better to begin by studying myth in tradi-tional and archaic societies, reserving for later consideration the mythologies of people who have played an important role in history. The reason is that, despite modifications in the course of time, the myths of "primitives" still reflect a primordial condition. Then, too, in "primitive" societies myths are still living, still establish and justify all human conduct and activity. The role and function of these myths can still (or could until very recently) be minutely observed and described by ethnologists. In the case of each myth, as of each ritual, it has been possible to question the natives and to learn, at least partially, the significance that they accord to it. Obviously, these "living documents," recorded in the course of investigations conducted on the spot, do not solve all our difficulties. But they have the not inconsiderable advantage of helping us to pose the problem in the right way, that is, to set myth in its original socioreligious context.

Attempt at a definition of myth

It would be hard to find a definition of myth that would be acceptable to all scholars and at the same time intelligible to nonspecialists. Then, too, is it even possible to find *one* definition that will cover all the types and functions of myths in all traditional and archaic societies? Myth is an extremely complex cultural reality, which can be approached and interpreted from various and complementary viewpoints.

Speaking for myself, the definition that seems least inadequate because most embracing is this: Myth narrates a sacred history; it relates an event that took place in primordial Time, the fabled time of the "beginnings." In other words, myth tells how, through the deeds of Supernatural Beings, a reality came into existence, be it the whole of reality, the Cosmos, or only a fragment of reality—an island, a species of plant, a particular kind of human behavior, an institution. Myth, then, is always an account of a "creation"; it relates how something was produced, began to *be*. Myth tells only of that which *really* happened, which manifested itself completely. The actors in myths are Supernatural Beings. They are known primarily by what they did in the transcendent times of the "beginnings." Hence myths disclose their creative activity and reveal the sacredness (or simply the "supernaturalness") of their works. In short, myths describe the various and sometimes dramatic breakthroughs of the sacred (or the "supernatural") into the World. It is this sudden breakthrough of the sacred that really *establishes* the World and makes it what it is today. Furthermore, it is as a result of the intervention of Supernatural Beings that man himself is what he is today, a mortal, sexed, and cultural being.

We shall later have occasion to enlarge upon and refine these few preliminary indications, but at this point it is necessary to emphasize a fact that we consider essential: the myth is regarded as a sacred story, and hence a "true history," because it always deals with *realities*. The cosmogonic myth is "true" because the existence of the World is there to prove it; the myth of the origin of death is equally true because man's mortality proves it, and so on.

Because myth relates the *gesta* of Supernatural Beings and the manifestation of their sacred powers, it becomes the exemplary model for all significant human activities. When the missionary and ethnologist C. Strehlow asked the Australian Arunta why they performed certain ceremonies, the answer was always: "Because the ancestors so commanded it."[1] The

---

[1] C. Strehlow, *Die Aranda-und-Loritja-Stämme in Zentral-Australien,* vol. III, p. i; cf. Lucien Lévy-Bruhl, *La mythologie primitive* (Paris,

Kai of New Guinea refused to change their way of living and working, and they explained: "It was thus that the Nemu (the Mythical Ancestors) did, and we do likewise."[2] Asked the reason for a particular detail in a ceremony, a Navaho chanter answered: "Because the Holy People did it that way in the first place."[3] We find exactly the same justification in the prayer that accompanies a primitive Tibetan ritual: "As it has been handed down from the beginning of earth's creation, so must we sacrifice. . . . As our ancestors in ancient times did—so do we now."[4] The same justification is alleged by the Hindu theologians and ritualists. "We must do what the gods did in the beginning" (*Satapatha Brāhmana,* VII, 2, 1, 4). "Thus the gods did; thus men do" (*Taittiriya Brāhmana,* I, 5, 9, 4).[5]

As we have shown elsewhere,[6] even the profane behavior and activities of man have their models in the deeds of the Supernatural Beings. Among the Navahos "women are required to sit with their legs under them and to one side, men with their legs crossed in front of them, because it is said that in the beginning Changing Woman and the Monster Slayer sat in these positions."[7] According to the mythical traditions

1935), p. 123. See also T. G. H. Strehlow, *Aranda Traditions* (Melbourne University Press, 1947), p. 6.

[2] C. Keysser, quoted by Richard Thurnwald, *Die Eingeborenen Australiens und der Südseeinseln* (=Religionsgeschichtliches Lesebuch, 8, Tübingen, 1927), p. 28.

[3] Clyde Kluckhohn, "Myths and Rituals: A General Theory," *Harvard Theological Review,* vol. 35 (1942), p. 66. Cf. *ibid.* for other examples.

[4] Matthias Hermanns, *The Indo-Tibetans* (Bombay, 1954), pp. 66 ff.

[5] See M. Eliade, *The Myth of the Eternal Return* (New York, 1954), pp. 21 ff.

[6] *Ibid.,* pp. 27 f.

[7] Clyde Kluckhohn, *op. cit.,* quoting W. W. Hill, *The Agricultural and Hunting Methods of the Navaho Indians* (New Haven, 1938), p. 179.

of an Australian tribe, the Karadjeri, all their customs, and indeed all their behavior, were established in the "Dream Time" by two Supernatural Beings, the Bagadjimbiri (for example, the way to cook a certain cereal or to hunt an animal with a stick, the particular position to be taken when urinating, and so on).[8]

There is no need to add further examples. As we showed in *The Myth of the Eternal Return,* and as will become still clearer later, the foremost function of myth is to reveal the exemplary models for all human rites and all significant human activities—diet or marriage, work or education, art or wisdom. This idea is of no little importance for understanding the man of archaic and traditional societies, and we shall return to it later.

"True stories" and "false stories"

We may add that in societies where myth is still alive the natives carefully distinguish myths—"true stories"—from fables or tales, which they call "false stories." The Pawnee "differentiate 'true stories' from 'false stories,' and include among the 'true' stories in the first place all those which deal with the beginnings of the world; in these the actors are divine beings, supernatural, heavenly, or astral. Next come those tales which relate the marvellous adventures of the national hero, a youth of humble birth who became the saviour of his people, freeing them from monsters, delivering them from famine and other disasters, and performing other noble a⌐

[8] Cf. M. Eliade, *Myths, Dreams and Mysteries* (New York, 1960), pp. 191 ff.

beneficent deeds. Last come the stories which have to do with the world of the medicine-men and explain how such-and-such a sorcerer got his superhuman powers, how such-and-such an association of shamans originated, and so on. The 'false' stories are those which tell of the far from edifying adventures and exploits of Coyote, the prairie-wolf. Thus in the 'true' stories we have to deal with the holy and the supernatural, while the 'false' ones on the other hand are of profane content, for Coyote is extremely popular in this and other North American mythologies in the character of a trickster, deceiver, sleight-of-hand expert and accomplished rogue."[9]

Similarly, the Cherokee distinguish between sacred myths (cosmogony, creation of the stars, origin of death) and profane stories, which explain, for example, certain anatomical or physiological peculiarities of animals. The same distinction is found in Africa. The Herero consider the stories that relate the beginnings of the different groups of the tribe "true" because they report facts that *really* took place, while the more or less humorous tales have no foundation. As for the natives of Togo, they look on their origin myths as "absolutely real."[10]

This is why myths cannot be related without regard to circumstances. Among many tribes they are not recited before women or children, that is, before the uninitiated. Usually the old teachers communicate the myths to the neophytes during their period of isolation in the bush, and this forms part of their initiation. R. Piddington says of the Karadjeri:

[9] R. Pettazzoni, *Essays on the History of Religions* (Leiden, 1954), pp. 11–12. Cf. also Werner Müller, *Die Religionen der Waldlandindianer Nordamerikas* (Berlin, 1956), p. 42.
[10] R. Pettazzoni, *op. cit.*, p. 13.

"the sacred myths that women may not know are concerned principally with the cosmogony and especially with the institution of the initiation ceremonies."[11]

Whereas "false stories" can be told anywhere and at any time, myths must not be recited except *during a period of sacred time* (usually in autum or winter, and only at night).[12] This custom has survived even among peoples who have passed beyond the archaic stage of culture. Among the Turco-Mongols and the Tibetans the epic songs of the Gesar cycle can be recited only at night and in winter. "The recitation is assimilated to a powerful charm. It helps to obtain all sorts of advantages, particularly success in hunting and war. . . . Before the recitation begins, a space is prepared by being powdered with roasted barley flour. The audience sit around it. The bard recites the epic for several days. They say that in former times the hoofprints of Gesar's horse appeared in the prepared space. Hence the recitation brought the real presence of the hero."[13]

What myths reveal

This distinction made by natives between "true stories" and "false stories" is significant. Both categories of narratives present "histories," that is, relate a series of events that took place in a distant and fabulous past. Although the actors in myths are usually Gods and Supernatural Beings, while those in tales are heroes or miraculous animals, all the actors share the

[11] R. Piddington, quoted by L. Lévy-Bruhl, p. 115. On initiation ceremonies, cf. Eliade, *Birth and Rebirth* (New York, 1958).

[12] See examples in R. Pettazzoni, *op. cit.,* p. 14, n. 15.

[13] R. A. Stein, *Recherches sur l'épopée et le barde au Tibet* (Paris, 1959), pp. 318–319.

common trait that they do not belong to the everyday world. Nevertheless, the natives have felt that the two kinds of "stories" are basically different. For everything that the myths relate *concerns them directly,* while the tales and fables refer to events that, even when they have caused changes in the World (cf. the anatomical or physiological peculiarities of certain animals), have not altered the human condition as such.[14]

Myths, that is, narrate not only the origin of the World, of animals, of plants, and of man, but also all the primordial events in consequence of which man became what he is to-day—mortal, sexed, organized in a society, obliged to work in order to live, and working in accordance with certain rules. If the World *exists,* if man *exists,* it is because Supernatural Beings exercised creative powers in the "beginning." But after the cosmogony and the creation of man other events occurred, and man *as he is today* is the direct result of those mythical events, *he is constituted by those events.* He is mortal because something happened *in illo tempore.* If that thing had not happened, man would not be mortal—he would have gone on existing indefinitely, like rocks; or he might have changed his skin periodically like snakes, and hence would have been able to renew his life, that is, begin it over again indefinitely. But the myth of the origin of death narrates what happened *in illo tempore,* and, in telling the incident, explains *why* man is mortal.

[14] Of course, what is considered a "true story" in one tribe can become a "false story" in a neighboring tribe. "Demythicization" is a process that is already documented in the archaic stages of culture. What is important is the fact that "primitives" are always aware of the difference between myths ("true stories") and tales or legends ("false stories"). Cf. Appendix I ("Myths and Fairy Tales").

Similarly, a certain tribe live by fishing—because in mythical times a Supernatural Being taught their ancestors to catch and cook fish. The myth tells the story of the first fishery, and, in so doing, at once reveals a superhuman act, teaches men how to perform it, and, finally, explains why this particular tribe must procure their food in this way.

It would be easy to multiply examples. But those already given show why, for archaic man, myth is a matter of primary importance, while tales and fables are not. Myth teaches him the primordial "stories" that have constituted him existentially; and everything connected with his existence and his legitimate mode of existence in the Cosmos concerns him directly.

We shall presently see what consequences this peculiar conception had for the behavior of archaic man. We may note that, just as modern man considers himself to be constituted by History, the man of the archaic societies declares that he is the result of a certain number of mythical events. Neither regards himself as "given," "made" once and for all, as, for example, a tool is made once and for all. A modern man might reason as follows: I am what I am today because a certain number of things have happened to me, but those things were possible only because agriculture was discovered some eight to nine thousand years ago and because urban civilizations developed in the ancient Near East, because Alexander the Great conquered Asia and Augustus founded the Roman Empire, because Galileo and Newton revolutionized the conception of the universe, thus opening the way to scientific discoveries and laying the groundwork for the rise of industrial civilization, because the French Revolution occurred and the ideas of freedom, democracy, and social justice shook the Western world to its foundations after the Napoleonic wars—and so on.

Similarly, a "primitive" could say: I am what I am today because a series of events occurred before I existed. But he would at once have to add: events that took place *in mythical times* and therefore make up a *sacred history* because the actors in the drama are not men but Supernatural Beings. In addition, while a modern man, though regarding himself as the result of the course of Universal History, does not feel obliged to know the whole of it, the man of the archaic societies is not only obliged to remember mythical history but also to *re-enact* a large part of it periodically. It is here that we find the greatest difference between the man of the archaic societies and modern man: the irreversibility of events, which is the characteristic trait of History for the latter, is not a fact to the former.

Constantinople was conquered by the Turks in 1453 and the Bastille fell on July 14, 1789. Those events are irreversible. To be sure, July 14th having become the national holiday of the French Republic, the taking of the Bastille is commemorated annually, but the historical event itself is not re-enacted.[15] For the man of the archaic societies, on the contrary, what happened *ab origine* can be repeated by the power of rites. For him, then, the essential thing is to know the myths. It is essential not only because the myths provide him with an explanation of the World and his own mode of being in the World, but above all because, by recollecting the myths, by re-enacting them, he is able to repeat what the Gods, the Heroes, or the Ancestors did *ab origine*. To know the myths

---

[15] Cf. *Myths, Dreams and Mysteries,* pp. 30 ff.

is to learn the secret of the origin of things. In other words, one learns not only how things came into existence but also where to find them and how to make them reappear when they disappear.

What "knowing the myths" means

Australian totemic myths usually consist in a rather monotonous narrative of peregrinations by mythical ancestors or totemic animals. They tell how, in the "Dream Time" (*alcheringa*)—that is, in mythical time—these Supernatural Beings made their appearance on earth and set out on long journeys, stopping now and again to change the landscape or to produce certain animals and plants, and finally vanished underground. But knowledge of these myths is essential for the life of the Australians. The myths teach them how to repeat the creative acts of the Supernatural Beings, and hence how to ensure the multiplication of such-and-such an animal or plant.

These myths are told to the neophytes during their initiation. Or rather, they are "performed," that is, re-enacted. "When the youths go through the various initiation ceremonies, [their instructors] perform a series of ceremonies before them; these, though carried out exactly like those of the cult proper —except for certain characteristic particulars—do not aim at the multiplication and growth of the totem in question but are simply intended to show those who are to be raised, or have just been raised, to the rank of men the way to perform these cult rituals."[16]

We see, then, that the "story" narrated by the myth con-

[16] C. Strehlow, *op. cit.,* vol. III, pp. 1–2; L. Lévy-Bruhl, *op. cit.,* p. 123. On puberty initiations in Australia, cf. *Birth and Rebirth,* pp. 4 ff.

stitutes a "knowledge" which is esoteric, not only because it is secret and is handed on during the course of an initiation but also because the "knowledge" is accompanied by a magico-religious power. For knowing the origin of an object, an animal, a plant, and so on is equivalent to acquiring a magical power over them by which they can be controlled, multiplied, or reproduced at will. Erland Nordenskiöld has reported some particularly suggestive examples from the Cuna Indians. According to their beliefs, the lucky hunter is the one who knows the origin of the game. And if certain animals can be tamed, it is because the magicians know the secret of their creation. Similarly, you can hold red-hot iron or grasp a poisonous snake if you know the origin of fire and snakes. Nordenskiöld writes that "in one Cuna village, Tientiki, there is a fourteen-year-old boy who can step into fire unharmed simply because he knows the charm of the creation of fire. Perez often saw people grasp red-hot iron and others tame snakes."[17]

This is a quite widespread belief, not connected with any particular type of culture. In Timor, for example, when a rice field sprouts, someone who knows the mythical traditions concerning rice goes to the spot. "He spends the night there in the plantation hut, reciting the legends that explain how man came to possess rice [origin myth]. . . . Those who do this are not priests."[18] Reciting its origin myth compels the rice to come up as fine and vigorous and thick as it was when *it appeared for the first time*. The officiant does not remind it of how it was created in order to "instruct" it, to teach it

[17] E. Nordenskiöld, "Faiseurs de miracles et voyants chez les Indiens Cuna," *Revista del Instituto de Etnologia* (Tucumán), vol. II (1932), p. 464; Lévy-Bruhl, *op. cit.*, p. 118.
[18] A. C. Kruyt, quoted by Lévy-Bruhl, *op. cit.*, p. 119.

how it should behave. He *magically compels it to go back to the beginning,* that is, to repeat its exemplary creation.

The *Kalevala* relates that the old Väinämöinen cut himself badly while building a boat. Then "he began to weave charms in the manner of all magic healers. He chanted the birth of the cause of his wound, but he could not remember the words that told of the beginning of iron, those very words which might heal the gap ripped open by the blue steel blade." Finally, after seeking the help of other magicians, Väinämöinen cried: "I now remember the origin of iron! and he began the tale as follows: Air is the first of mothers. Water is the eldest of brothers, fire the second and iron the youngest of the three. Ukko, the great Creator, separated earth from water and drew soil into marine lands, but iron was yet unborn. Then he rubbed his palms together upon his left knee. Thus were born three nature maidens to be the mothers of iron."[19] It should be noted that, in this example, the myth of the origin of iron forms part of the cosmogonic myth and, in a sense, continues it. This is an extremely important and specific characteristic of origin myths, and we shall study it in the next chapter.

The idea that a remedy does not act unless its origin is known is extremely widespread. To quote Erland Nordenskiöld again: "Every magical chant must be preceded by an incantation telling the origin of the remedy used, otherwise it does not act. . . . For the remedy or the healing chant to have its effect, it is necessary to know the origin of the plant, the manner in which the first woman gave birth to it."[20]

[19] Aili Kolehmainen Johnson, *Kalevala. A Prose translation from the Finnish* (Hancock, Mich., 1950), pp. 53 ff.

[20] E. Nordenskiöld, "La conception de l'âme chez les Indiens Cuna de

In the Na-khi ritual chants published by J. F. Rock it is expressly stated: "If one does not relate . . . the origin of the medicine, to slander it is not proper."[21] Or: "Unless its origin is related one should not speak about it."[22]

We shall see in the following chapter that, as in the Väinämöinen myth given above, the origin of remedies is closely connected with the history of the origin of the World. It should be noted, however, that this is only part of a general conception, which may be formulated as follows: *A rite cannot be performed unless its "origin" is known, that is, the myth that tells how it was performed for the first time.* During the funeral service the Na-khi shaman chants:

"Now we will escort the deceased and again experience bitterness;
We will again dance and suppress the demons.
If it is not told whence the dance originated
One must not speak about it.
Unless one know the origin of the dance
One cannot dance."[23]

This is curiously reminiscent of what the Uitoto told Preuss: "Those are the words (myths) of our father, his very words. Thanks to those words we dance, and there would be no dance if he had not given them to us."[24]

In most cases it is not enough to *know* the origin myth, one must *recite* it; this, in a sense, is a proclamation of one's

l'Isthme de Panama," *Journal des Américanistes,* N.S., vol. 24 (1932), pp. 5–30, 14.

[21] J. F. Rock, *The Na-Khi Nâga Cult and related ceremonies* (Rome, 1952), vol. II, p. 474.

[22] *Ibid.,* vol. II, p. 487.

[23] J. F. Rock, *Zhi-mä funeral ceremony of the Na-Khi* (Vienna Mödling, 1955), p. 87.

[24] K. T. Preuss, *Religion und Mythologie der Uitoto,* vols. I–II (Göttingen, 1921–23), p. 625.

knowledge, *displays* it. But this is not all. He who recites or performs the origin myth is thereby steeped in the sacred atmosphere in which these miraculous events took place. The mythical time of origins is a "strong" time because it was transfigured by the active, creative presence of the Supernatural Beings. By reciting the myths one reconstitutes that fabulous time and hence in some sort becomes "contemporary" with the events described, one is in the presence of the Gods or Heroes. As a summary formula we might say that by "living" the myths one emerges from profane, chronological time and enters a time that is of a different quality, a "sacred" Time at once primordial and indefinitely recoverable. This function of myth, which we have emphasized in our *Myth of the Eternal Return* (especially pp. 35 ff.), will appear more clearly in the course of the following analyses.

Structure and function of myths

These few preliminary remarks are enough to indicate certain characteristic qualities of myth. In general it can be said that myth, as experienced by archaic societies, (1) constitutes the History of the acts of the Supernaturals; (2) that this History is considered to be absolutely *true* (because it is concerned with realities) and *sacred* (because it is the work of the Supernaturals); (3) that myth is always related to a "creation," it tells how something came into existence, or how a pattern of behavior, an institution, a manner of working were established; this is why myths constitute the paradigms for all significant human acts; (4) that by knowing the myth one knows the "origin" of things and hence can control and manipulate them at will; this is not an "external," "abstract" knowledge but a knowledge that one "experiences" ritually, either by ceremonially recounting the myth or by performing the ritual for which it is the justification; (5) that in one way or another one "lives" the myth, in the sense that one is seized by the sacred, exalting power of the events recollected or re-enacted.

"Living" a myth, then, implies a genuinely "religious" experience, since it differs from the ordinary experience of everyday life. The "religiousness" of this experience is due to the fact that one re-enacts fabulous, exalting, significant events, one again witnesses the creative deeds of the Supernaturals; one ceases to exist in the everyday world and enters a transfigured, auroral world impregnated with the Supernaturals' presence. What is involved is not a commemoration of mythical events but a reiteration of them. The protagonists of the myth are made present, one becomes their contemporary. This also implies that one is no longer living in chronological time, but in the primordial Time, the Time when the event *first took place*. This is why we can use the term the "strong time" of myth; it is the prodigious, "sacred" time when something *new, strong,* and *significant* was manifested. To re-experience that time, to re-enact it as often as possible, to witness again the spectacle of the divine works, to meet with the Supernaturals and relearn their creative lesson is the desire that runs like a pattern through all the ritual reiterations of myths. In short, myths reveal that the World, man, and life have a supernatural origin and history, and that this history is significant, precious, and exemplary.

I cannot conclude this chapter better than by quoting the classic passages in which Bronislav Malinowski undertook to show the nature and function of myth in primitive societies.

"Studied alive, myth . . . is not an explanation in satisfaction of a scientific interest, but a narrative resurrection of a primeval reality, told in satisfaction of deep religious wants, moral cravings, social submissions, assertions, even practical requirements. Myth fulfills in primitive culture an indispensable function: it expresses, enhances, and codifies belief; it safeguards and enforces morality; it vouches for the efficiency of ritual and contains practical rules for the guidance of man. Myth is thus a vital ingredient of human civilisation; it is not an idle tale, but a hard-worked active force; it is not an intellectual explanation or an artistic imagery, but a pragmatic charter of primitive faith and moral wisdom. . . . These stories . . . are to the natives a statement of a primeval, greater, and more relevant reality, by which the present life, fates and activities of mankind are determined, the knowledge of which supplies man with the motive for ritual and moral actions, as well as with indications as to how to perform them."[25]

[25] B. Malinowski, *Myth in Primitive Psychology* (1926; reprinted in *Magic, Science and Religion* [New York, 1955], pp. 101, 108).

II.

Magic and Prestige of "Origins"

Origin myths and cosmogonic myths

EVERY mythical account of the *origin* of anything presupposes and continues the cosmogony. From the structural point of view, origin myths can be homologized with the cosmogonic myth. The creation of the World being *the* pre-eminent instance of creation, the cosmogony becomes the exemplary model for "creation" of every kind. This does not mean that the origin myth imitates or copies the cosmogonic model, for no concerted and systematized reflection is involved. But every new appearance—an animal, a plant, an institution—implies the existence of a World. Even when it is a matter of explaining how, starting from a different state of things, the present situation was reached (for example, how the Sky was separated from the Earth, or how man became mortal), the "World" was already there, even though its structure was different, though it was not yet *our* world. Every origin myth narrates and justifies a "new situation"—new in the sense that it did not exist *from the beginning of the World.* Origin myths continue and complete the cosmogonic myth; they tell how the world was changed, made richer or poorer.

This is why some origin myths begin by outlining a cosmogony. The history of the great families and dynasties of

Tibet opens by rehearsing the birth of the Cosmos from an Egg. "From the essence of the five primordial elements a great egg came forth. . . . Eighteen eggs came forth from the yolk of that great egg. The egg in the middle of the eighteen eggs, a conch egg, separated from the others. From this conch egg limbs grew, and then the five senses, all perfect, and it became a boy of such extraordinary beauty that he seemed the fulfillment of every wish (*yid la smon*). Hence he was named King Ye-smon. Queen Tchu-lchag, his wife, gave birth to a son who could transform himself through magic, Dbang-ldan."[1] Then the genealogy proceeds, relating the origins and histories of the various clans and dynasties.

The Polynesian genealogical chants begin in the same way. The Hawaiian ritual text known as the Kumulipo is "a genealogical prayer chant linking the royal family to which it belonged not only to the primary gods belonging to the whole people and worshipped in common with allied Polynesian groups, not only to deified chiefs born into the living world, the Ao, within the family line, but to the stars in the heavens and the plants and animals useful to life on earth. . . ."[2] And in fact the chant begins by evoking

> "The time when the earth was hotly changed
> The time when the heavens separately changed
> The time when the sun was rising
> To give light to the moon," etc.[3]

[1] Ariane Macdonald, "La Naissance du Monde au Tibet" (in: *Sources Orientales* [Paris, 1959], vol. I, p. 428). Cf. also R. A. Stein, *Recherches sur l'épopée et le barde au Tibet*, p. 464.

[2] Martha Warner Beckwith, *The Kumulipo. A Hawaiian Creation Chant* (University of Chicago Press, 1951), p. 7.

[3] *Ibid.*, p. 45. "The rebirth of light each day, the annual return of the sun from the south to revivify earth, serve not only as symbols of this

Such ritual genealogical chants are composed by the bards when the princess is pregnant, and they are communicated to the *hula* dancers to be learned by heart. The dancers, men and women, dance and recite the chant continuously until the child is born. It is as if the embryological development of the future chief were accompanied by a recapitulation of the cosmogony, the history of the World, and the history of the tribe. The gestation of a chief is the occasion for a symbolic "re-creation" of the World. The recapitulation is at once a reminder and a ritual reactualization, through song and dance, of the essential mythical events that have taken place since the Creation.

Similar concepts and rituals are found among the primitive peoples of India. Among the Santali, for example, the *guru* recites the cosmogonic myth for each individual, but only on two occasions. The first time is "when a Santal is granted full social rights. . . . On this occasion the *guru* recites the history of humanity from the creation of the world and ends by narrating the birth of the person for whom the rite is being performed." The same ceremony is repeated during the funeral service, but this time the *guru* ritually transfers the soul of the deceased to the other world.[4] Among the Gonds and the Baigas, when the rituals in honor of Dharti Mata and Thakur Deo are performed, the priest recites the cosmogonic myth and reminds the audience of the important

---

human birth but as that birth's direct pattern or even its determining factor in the perfectuation of the race. . . . As Wakea, the sky world, bursts the bonds of night and rises out of the womb of waters where it has lain in darkness, so the child bursts the sheath where it lay within its mother's womb and emerges into the light of reasoning human life" (*ibid.,* pp. 182–183).

[4] P. O. Bodding, "Les Santals," *Journal Asiatique,* 1932, pp. 58 ff.

role that their tribe played in the creation of the World.[5]
When the Munda magicians drive out evil spirits they recite
the mythological songs of the Assur. The Assur inaugurated
a new epoch not only for the Gods and spirits but also for
human beings; hence the history of their exploits may be
regarded as part of the cosmogonic myth.[6]

Among the Bhils the situation is somewhat different. Only
one of their curative magical chants has the nature of a cosmogonic myth—*The Lord Song*. But in point of fact the
majority of them are origin myths. *The Song of Kasumor
Dâmor,* for example, which is believed to cure all illnesses,
narrates the migrations of the Dâmor group of the Bhils
from Gujerat to the southern part of Central India.[7] It is,
then, the myth of the territorial settling of the group—in
other words, the history of a *new beginning,* a counterpart to
the Creation of the World. Other magical songs reveal the
origin of sicknesses.[8] The myths that they tell are full of adventures and end by recounting the circumstances under which
sicknesses appeared—an event which, of course, changed the
structure of the world.

The role of myths in healing

One detail in the healing ritual of the Bhils is of particular
interest. The magician "purifies" the space beside the patient's

[5] V. Elwin, *The Baiga* (London, 1939), p. 305; W. Koppers, *Die Bhil
in zentral-indien* (Vienna, 1948), p. 242.

[6] W. Koppers, *Die Bhil,* p. 242; J. Hoffmann and A. van Emelen,
Encyclopaedia Mundarica (Patna, 1930), vol. III, p. 739.

[7] L. Jungblut, "Magic Songs of the Bhils of Jhabua State," *Interna-
tionales Archiv für Ethnographie,* vol. XLIII (1943), p. 6.

[8] *Ibid.,* pp. 35 ff., 59 ff.

bed and draws a *mandol* with corn flour. At the center of
the design he puts the house of Isvor and Bhagwân, together
with their figures. This drawing is preserved until the patient
is completely cured.[9] The term *"mandol"* itself testifies to an
Indian origin. This is, of course, the *mandala,* a complex
design that plays a large part in Indo-Tibetan tantric rites.
But the *mandala* is primarily an *imago mundi;* it represents
the Cosmos in miniature and, at the same time, the pantheon.
Its construction is equivalent to a magical re-creation of the
world. Hence when the Bhil magician draws a *mandol* at the
patient's bedside he is repeating the cosmogony, even if
the ritual songs that he sings do not expressly refer to the
cosmogonic myth. The operation certainly has a therapeutic
purpose. Made symbolically contemporary with the Creation
of the World, the patient is immersed in the primordial fullness of life; he is penetrated by the gigantic forces that, *in
illo tempore,* made the Creation possible.

In this connection it is of interest to note that, among the
Navahos, the cosmogonic myth, followed by the myth of the
emergence of the first men from the bosom of the Earth,
is seldom recited except on the occasion of a cure or during
the initiation of a shaman. "All the ceremonies center around
a patient, Hatrali (one sung over), who may be sick or merely
sick in mind, i.e. frightened by a dream, or who may be
needing only a ceremony, in order to learn it in the course
of being initiated into full power of officiating in that chant
—for a Medicine Man cannot give a healing ceremony until
he has the ceremony given over him."[10] The ceremony also

[9] *Ibid.,* p. 5.
[10] Hasteen Klah, *Navajo Creation Myth: The Story of the Emergence*
(Santa Fe, 1942), p. 19. Cf. also *ibid.,* pp. 25 ff., 32 ff.

includes executing complex sand paintings, which symbolize
the various stages of Creation and the mythical history of the
gods, the ancestors, and mankind. These drawings (which
strangely resemble the Indo-Tibetan *mandala*) successively
re-enact the events which took place in mythical times. As
he hears the cosmogonic myth and then the origin myths
recited and contemplates the sand paintings, the patient is
projected out of profane time into the fullness of primordial
Time; he is carried "back" to the origin of the World and is
thus present at the cosmogony.

The close connection between the cosmogonic myth, the
myth of the origin of a sickness and its remedy, and the ritual
of magical healing is admirably exemplified among the Na-
khi, a people belonging to the Tibetan family but who for
many centuries have lived in southeastern China, especially
in Yunnan province. According to their traditions, in the beginning the Universe was duly divided between the Nagas
and mankind, but later they became enemies. In their anger
the Nagas afflicted the world with sicknesses, sterility, and
every kind of scourge. The Nagas can also steal men's souls,
making them sick. If they are not ritually reconciled, the
victim dies. But the priest-shaman (*dto-mba*), by the power
of his magical charms, can force the Nagas to free the souls
that they have stolen and imprisoned.[11] The shaman himself
can only fight the Nagas because the First Shaman, Dto-mba,
first attacked them in mythical times with the help of Garuda.
Strictly speaking, the healing ritual consists in the solemn
recital of this primordial event. As a text translated by Rock
expressly says: "If the origin of Garuda is not related, then

[11] J. F. Rock, *The Na-khi Nâga Cult and related ceremonies* (Rome,
1952), vol. I, pp. 9–10.

one must not speak of him."[12] The shaman, then, recites the origin myth of Garuda. He tells how eggs were created by magic on Mount Kailasa and how from these eggs were born the Garudas, who later came down to the plain to defend men against the sicknesses caused by the Nagas. But before relating the birth of the Garudas, the ritual chant briefly rehearses the Creation of the World: "At the time when heaven came forth, the sun, moon, stars and planets, and the earth was spread out; when the mountains, valleys, trees and rocks came forth . . . at that time there came forth the Nagas and dragons, etc."[13]

Most of these medical ritual chants begin by evoking the cosmogony. Here is an example: "In the beginning, at the time when the heavens, sun, moon, stars, planets and the land had not yet appeared, when nothing had yet come forth, etc."[14] Then comes the creation of the world, the birth of the demons and the appearance of sicknesses, and finally the epiphany of the Primordial Shaman, Dto-mba, who provided the necessary medicines. Another text[15] begins by evoking the mythical age: "In the beginning, when everything was indistinguishable, etc." and then goes on to describe the birth of the Nagas and Garudas. Then comes the origin of the sickness (for, as we saw earlier, "if one does not relate of the origin of the medicine, to slander it is not proper"), the means by which it is propagated from generation to generation, and finally the struggle between the demons and the shaman: "The ghost gives illness to the teeth and mouth, by shooting off the arrow, the *dto-mba* pulls out the arrow, etc.; the demon

[12] *Ibid.*, vol. I, p. 98.
[13] *Ibid.*, vol. I, p. 97.
[14] *Ibid.*, vol. I, p. 108.
[15] *Ibid.*, vol. II, pp. 386 ff.

gives illness to the body, by shooting off the arrow into the body, the *dto-mba* pulls it out, etc."[16]

Another ritual song begins: "One must relate . . . the origin of the medicine, otherwise one cannot speak about it. At the time when heaven, the stars, sun and moon and the planets came forth, and the earth appeared," etc., "at that time was born Ts'o-dze-p'er-ddu."[17] Then comes a very long myth explaining the origin of medicines: away from home for three days, on his return Ts'o-dze-p'er-ddu finds his parents dead. He decides to go in search of a medicine that will prevent death and journeys to the country of the Chief of Spirits. After many adventures he steals the miraculous medicines, but, pursued by the spirit, he falls to the ground and the medicines are scattered, giving birth to medicinal plants.

Reiteration of the cosmogony

Some of the texts published by Hermanns are even more enlightening. In the course of a healing ritual the shaman not only summarizes the cosmogony but also invokes God and *implores him to create the World anew*. One of these prayers begins, "The earth was created, the water was created, the whole world was created. The millet beer offering *chi* and the rice offering *so* were created . . ." and ends with the summons, "Come hither, ye spirits."[18] Another text gives "the genesis of *chi*, the genesis of the intoxicating drink *dyö*. This arose from an old tradition. The place of origin is where the Sang li and Sang log trees originated. In the interest of

[16] *Ibid.,* vol. II, p. 489.
[17] *Ibid.,* vol. I, pp. 279 ff.
[18] M. Hermanns, *The Indo-Tibetans,* pp. 66 ff.

the whole world and for our use, O messenger of God, come hither. Tak bo thing, the wonder-power-god, came down for the creation of the world. *Now again come down for the creation of the world.*"[19] It is clear that to prepare the ritual beverages *chi* and *dyö* it is necessary to know the myth of their origin, which is closely connected with the cosmogonic myth. But, even more significantly, the Creator is asked to come down again for a new creation of the World, for the patient's benefit.

We see that in these magical medical chants the *myth of the origin of the medicines* is always made an integral part of the *cosmogonic myth.* In the preceding chapter we cited some examples to show that, in primitive therapeutics, a remedy becomes efficacious only if its origin is ritually recalled in the patient's presence. Many Near Eastern and European incantations contain the history of the sickness or of the demon who brought it on, and at the same time recall the mythical moment when a divinity or a saint succeeded in conquering the scourge. An Assyrian incantation against toothache recalls that "after Anu made the heavens, the heavens made the earth, the earth made the rivers, the rivers made the canals, the canals made the pools, the pools made the Worm." And the Worm goes "weeping" to Shamash and Ea, and asks them what it will be given to eat, to "destroy." The Gods offer it fruits, but the Worm demands human teeth. "Since thou hast spoken thus, O Worm, may Ea break thee with his powerful hand!"[20] Here we witness (1) the creation of the world; (2)

---

[19] *Ibid.,* p. 69. Our italics.

[20] Campbell Thompson, *Assyrian Medical Texts* (London, 1923), p. 59. See also the mythical history of the charm against snakebite invented by Isis *in illo tempore,* in G. Roeder, *Urkunden zur Religion des alten Aegypten* (Jena, 1915), pp. 138 ff.

the birth of the Worm and of the sickness; (3) the primordial and paradigmatic curative act (destruction of the Worm by Ea). The therapeutic efficacy of the incantation lies in the fact that, recited ritually, it re-enacts the mythical time of "origins," not only the origin of the world but also that of toothache and its treatment.

Sometimes a solemn recitation of the cosmogonic myth is enough to cure certain sicknesses or imperfections. But, as we shall presently see, this application of the cosmogonic myth is only one among others. As the exemplary model for all "creation," the cosmogonic myth can help the patient to make a "new beginning" of his life. The *return to origins* gives the hope of a rebirth. Now, all the medical rituals we have been examining aim at a return to origins. We get the impression that for archaic societies life cannot be *repaired,* it can only be *re-created* by a return to sources. And the "source of sources" is the prodigious outpouring of energy, life, and fecundity that occurred at the Creation of the World.

All this is clearly apparent from the many ritual applications of the Polynesian cosmogonic myth. According to this myth, in the beginning there were only the Waters and Darkness. Io, the Supreme God, separated the Waters by the power of thought and of his words, and created the Sky and the Earth. He said: "Let the Waters be separated, let the Heavens be formed, let the Earth be!" These cosmogonic words of Io's, by virtue of which the World came into existence, are creative words, charged with sacred power. Hence men utter them whenever there is something to *do,* to *create.* They are repeated during the rite for making a sterile womb fecund, during the rite for curing body and mind, but also on the occasion of a death, of war, and of the recitation of genealogies. A contemporary Polynesian, Hare Hongi, puts it this way: "The words by which Io fashioned the Universe —that is to say, by which it was implanted and caused to produce a world of light—the same words are used in the ritual for implanting a child in a barren womb. The words by which Io caused light to shine in the darkness are used in rituals for cheering a gloomy and despondent heart, the feeble aged, the decrepit; for shedding light into secret places and matters, for inspiration in song-composing and in many other affairs, affecting man to despair in times of adverse war. For all such the ritual includes the words (used by Io) to overcome and dispel darkness."[21]

This is a remarkable text. It presents direct and incontrovertible testimony concerning the function of the cosmogonic myth in a traditional society. As we have just seen, this myth serves as the model for every kind of "creation"—the pro-creation of a child as well as the re-establishment of a military situation in jeopardy or of a psychic equilibrium threatened by melancholy and despair. This fact that the cosmogonic myth can be applied on various planes of reference seems to us especially significant. The man of the traditional societies feels the basic unity of all kinds of "deeds," "works," or "forms," whether they are biological, psychological, or historical. An unsuccessful war can be homologized with a sickness, with a dark, discouraged heart, with a sterile woman, with a poet's lack of inspiration, as with any other critical existential situation in which man is driven to despair. And all these negative, desperate, apparently irremediable situations are reversed by recitation of the cosmogonic myth, especially by the words by which Io brought forth the Universe

[21] E. S. C. Handy, *Polynesian Religion* (Honolulu, 1927), pp. 10–11.

and made light shine in the darkness. In other words, the cosmogony is the exemplary model for every creative situation: whatever man does is in some way a repetition of the pre-eminent "deed," the archetypal gesture of the Creator God, the Creation of the World.

As we have seen, the cosmogonic myth is also recited on the occasion of a death; for death, too, constitutes a new situation, which must be accepted and assumed without cavil if it is to be made creative. A death can be "botched" as a battle can be lost, as psychic equilibrium and joy in living can be destroyed. It is no less significant that among disastrous and negative situations Hare Hongi reckons not only impotence, sickness, and senility, but also lack of inspiration in poets, their inability to create or fitly recite poems and genealogies. It follows from this, first, that among the Polynesians poetic creation is homologized with every other important creation and, in addition—since Hare Hongi mentions reciting gene-alogies—that the poet's memory is itself a "work" and that the accomplishment of this "work" can be assured by solemn recitation of the cosmogonic myth.

We can understand why this myth stands so high in the estimation of the Polynesians. The cosmogony is the exemplary model for every kind of "doing": not only because the Cosmos is at once the ideal archetype of every creative situation and of every creation but also because the Cosmos is a divine work; hence it is sanctified even in its structure. By extension, whatever is perfect, "full," harmonious, fertile—in short, what-ever is "cosmicized," whatever resembles a Cosmos—is sacred. To do something well, to work, construct, create, structure, give form, in-form, form—all this comes down to bringing something into existence, giving it "life," and, in the last analysis, making it like the pre-eminently harmonious organism, the Cosmos. Now, to repeat, the Cosmos is the exemplary work of the Gods, it is their masterpiece.

This regarding the cosmogonic myth as the exemplary model for every "creation" is admirably illustrated by a custom of the Osage Indians. When a child is born among the Osages, "a man who had talked with the gods" is summoned. When he reaches the new mother's house he recites the history of the creation of the Universe and the terrestrial animals to the newborn infant. Not until this has been done is the baby given the breast. Later, when it wants to drink water, the same man—or sometimes another—is called in again. Once again he recites the Creation, ending with the origin of Water. When the child is old enough to take solid food the man "who had talked with the gods" comes once more and again recites the Creation, this time also relating the origin of grains and other foods.[22]

It would be hard to find a more eloquent example of the belief that each new birth represents a symbolic recapitulation of the cosmogony and of the tribe's mythical history. The object of this recapitulation is to introduce the newborn child ritually into the sacramental reality of the World and culture and thus to validate the new existence by announcing that it conforms with the mythical paradigms. But this is not all. The newborn child is also made a witness to a series of "beginnings." And one cannot "begin" anything unless one knows its "origin," how it first came into being. When it "begins" to suckle or to drink water or to eat solid food, the child is

[22] Alice C. Fletcher and F. La Flesche, *The Omaha Tribe* (Bureau of American Ethnology, 27th Annual Report, Washington, 1911), p. 116, n. *a*.

ritually projected into the time of "origin" when milk, water, and grains first appeared on earth.

The "return to origins"

The idea implicit in this belief is that *it is the first manifestation of a thing that is significant and valid,* not its successive epiphanies. Similarly, the child is taught not what its father and grandfather did but what was done for the first time by the Ancestors, in mythical Times. To be sure, the father and grandfather simply imitated the Ancestors; hence it might be thought that imitating the father would produce the same results. But to think this would be to disregard the essential role of the *Time of Origin,* which, as we have seen, is considered a "strong" time precisely because it was in some sort the "receptacle" for a *new creation.* The time that has passed between the *origin* and the present moment is neither "strong" nor "significant" (except, of course, for the periods during which the primordial Time has been re-enacted); and for this reason it is neglected or an attempt is made to abolish it.[23]

In this example we have a ritual in which the cosmogonic myths are recited for the benefit of an individual, as in the case of healers. But the "return to the origin" that makes it possible to relive the time when things were first manifested is an experience of primary importance for the archaic societies. We shall discuss it more than once in the course of the following pages. But here we may cite an example of the solemn recitation of the cosmogonic and origin myths in the collective festivals of Sumba Island. When events of impor-

[23] Cf. *The Myth of the Eternal Return,* ch. II and *passim.*

tance to the community occur—an abundant harvest, the death of some eminent person, etc.—a ceremonial house (*marapu*) is built and on this occasion the narrators recount the history of the Creation and the Ancestors. "In all these cases the narrators respectfully refer to 'the beginnings,' i.e. the inception of the principles of the very culture which should be preserved as the most valuable treasure. A remarkable fact of this ceremony is that the recital actually takes the form of an interchange of question-and-answer by two persons constituting as it were each other's counterpart, since they are singled out from two groups with a mutual exogamous connubial relationship. So these two spokesmen in those critical moments represent the total group together with the dead, and consequently the recital of the tribal myth (which should at the same time also be conceived as cosmogonical), will benefit the group as a whole."[24]

In other words, we here have collective rituals, performed at irregular intervals and including the construction of a cult house and the solemn recitation of origin myths of cosmogonic structure. The beneficiary is the whole community, including both the living and the dead. On the occasion of the re-presentation of the myths the entire community is renewed; it rediscovers its "sources," relives its "origins." The idea of a universal renewal brought about by the religious re-presentation of a cosmogonic myth is documented in many traditional societies. We have discussed it in *The Myth of the Eternal Return,* and we shall return to it in the following chapter. For the mythico-ritual scenario of the periodic renewal of the World can show us one of the most significant functions of

[24] C. T. Bertling, *Notes on Myth and Ritual in Southeast Asia* (The Hague, 1958), pp. 3–4.

myth, both in archaic cultures and in the earliest civilizations of the East.

Prestige of "beginnings"

The few examples we have given make it easier to perceive the relations between the cosmogonic myths and origin myths. First and most important is the fact that the origin myth frequently begins with a sketch of the cosmogony: the myth briefly summarizes the essential moments of the Creation of the World and then goes on to relate the genealogy of the royal family or the history of the tribe or the history of the origin of sicknesses and remedies, and so on.[25] In all these cases the origin myths continue and complete the cosmogonic myth. In the case of the ritual function of certain origin myths (in cures, for example, or, as among the Osages, myths intended to introduce the newborn infant into the sacrality of the World and society), we get the impression that their "powers" are due in part to their containing the rudiments of a cosmogony. This impression is confirmed by the fact that in some cultures (Polynesia, for example), the cosmogonic

[25] The custom persists even in developed societies possessing writing. S. N. Kramer remarks in regard to Sumerian texts: "The Sumerian poets usually began their myths or epic poems with a cosmological statement that had no direct bearing on the composition as a whole. Part of this introduction to 'Gilgamesh, Enkidu and the Nether World' consists of the following five lines:
> 'After Heaven had been moved away from earth,
> After earth had been separated from heaven,
> After the name of man had been fixed,
> After (the heaven-god) An carried off the heaven,
> After (the air-god) Enlil carried off the earth . . .'"
(S. N. Kramer, *From the Tablets of Sumer* [Indian Hills, Colo., 1956], p. 77.) So too in the Middle Ages many chroniclers began their local histories with the Creation of the World.

myth not only can possess an intrinsic therapeutic value but is also the exemplary model for every kind of "creation" and "doing."

This dependence of origin myths upon the cosmogonic myth is easier to explain if we bear in mind that, in both cases alike, there is a "beginning." But the absolute "beginning" is the Creation of the World. There is more than a mere theoretical curiosity here. It is not enough to *know* the "origin," it is necessary to re-establish the moment when such-and-such a thing was created. This finds expression in "going back" until the original, strong, sacred Time is recovered. And as we have seen and shall see more in detail later, recovering the primordial Time, which alone can ensure the complete renewal of the Cosmos, of life, and of society, is brought about primarily by re-establishing the "absolute beginning," that is, the Creation of the World.

Professor R. Pettazzoni has recently argued in favor of regarding the cosmogonic myth as a variant of the origin myth. "The result is that the creation-myth shares the same nature as the myth of beginnings. . . . Our analysis has allowed us to tear the creation-myth from its splendid isolation. It is no longer a *hapax genomenon,* but takes its place in a well-filled class of analogous phenomena, the myths of beginnings."[26] For the reasons just rehearsed we find it difficult to share this point of view. A new state of things always implies a preceding state, and the latter, in the last analysis, is the World. It is from this initial "totality" that the later modifications develop. The cosmic milieu in which one lives, limited as it may be, constitutes the "World"; its "origin" and

[26] R. Pettazzoni, *Essays on the History of Religions* (Leiden, 1954), pp. 27, 36.

"history" precede any other individual history. The mythical idea of the "origin" is part and parcel of the mystery of "creation." A thing has an "origin" because it was created, that is, because a power clearly manifested itself in the World, an event took place. In short, the *origin* of a thing accounts for its *creation*.

The proof that the cosmogonic myth is not a mere *variant* of the *species* "origin myth" resides in the fact that cosmogonies, as we have just seen, serve as the model for all kinds of "creations." The examples that we shall analyze in the following chapter will, we believe, further support this conclusion.

III.

Myths and Rites of Renewal

A. M. HOCART had observed that in Fiji the king's enthronement ceremony is called "creation of the world," "fashioning the land," or "creating the earth."[1] On the accession of a sovereign the cosmogony was symbolically repeated. The idea is rather widespread among agricultural peoples. According to a recent interpretation, the installation of the Indian king, the *rajasūya,* included re-creating the Universe. And in fact the various phases of the ritual successively brought about the future sovereign's reversion to the embryonic state, his gestation for a year, and his mystical rebirth as Cosmocrator, identified with both Prajāpati (the All-God) and the Cosmos.

The future sovereign's embryonic period corresponded to the maturation process of the Universe and, in all probability, was originally related to the ripening of crops. The second phase of the ritual completes the formation of the sovereign's new ("divine") body. The third phase of the *rajasūya* comprises a series of rites whose cosmogonic symbolism is sufficiently emphasized by the texts. The king raises his arms; he is symbolizing the raising of the *axis mundi.* When he is anointed he stands on the throne, arms lifted; he is incarnating the cosmic axis fixed in the navel of the Earth (that is,

[1] *The Myth of the Eternal Return,* pp. 80 ff.

the throne, the Center of the World) and touching the Heavens. The aspersion is connected with the Waters that come down from the Heavens along the *axis mundi* (that is, the king) to fertilize the Earth.[2]

In the historical period the *rajasūya* was performed only twice—the first time to consecrate the king and the second to ensure him universal sovereignty. But in protohistorical times the *rajasūya* was probably an annual rite, performed to regenerate the Cosmos.

Such was the case in Egypt. The coronation of a new pharaoh, Frankfort writes, "can be regarded as the creation of a new epoch after a dangerous interruption of the harmony between society and nature—a situation, therefore, which partakes of the quality of the creation of the universe. This is well illustrated by a text containing a curse on the king's enemies who are compared with Apophis, the snake of darkness whom Re destroys at dawn. But there is a curious addition to the comparison: 'They will be like the serpent Apophis on New Year's morn.' The qualification 'on New Year's morn' can only be explained as an intensification: the snake is defeated at every sunrise, but the New Year celebrates creation and daily renewal as well as the opening of the new annual cycle."[3]

It is clear how the cosmogonic scenario of the New Year can be incorporated into the coronation ceremony of a king. The two ritual systems pursue the same end—cosmic renewal. "But the *renovatio* accomplished at the coronation of a king had important consequences in the later history of humanity.

---

[2] M. Eliade, "Dimensions religieuses du renouvellement cosmique," *Eranos-Jahrbuch* (Zurich, 1960), vol. XXVIII, pp. 269 ff.

[3] H. Frankfort, *Kingship and the Gods* (Chicago, 1948), p. 150.

On the one hand, the ceremonies of renewal become movable, break away from the rigid frame of the calendar; on the other, the king becomes in a manner responsible for the stability, the fecundity, and the prosperity of the entire Cosmos. This is as much as to say that universal renewal is no longer bound to the cosmic rhythm and is connected instead with historical persons and events."[4]

Renewing the World

It is easy to understand why the installation of a king repeated the cosmogony or took place at the New Year. The king was believed to renew the entire Cosmos. The greatest of renewals takes place at the New Year, when a new time cycle is inaugurated. But the *renovatio* effected by the New Year ritual is, basically, a reiteration of the cosmogony. Each New Year begins the Creation over again. And it is by myths —both cosmogonic myths and origin myths—that man is reminded how the World was created and what happened afterward.

The world is always "our world," the world in which one lives. And although the mode of being of human existence is the same among the Australians as among modern Westerners, the cultural contexts in which human existence is apprehended vary widely. It is obvious, for example, that the "World" of

[4] M. Eliade, *op. cit.*, pp. 270–271. "It is in this conception that we find the source for future historical and political eschatologies. For in the course of time cosmic renewal, the 'Salvation' of the World, came to be expected from a certain type of King or Hero or Saviour or even political leader. Although in strongly secularized form, the modern world still keeps the eschatological hope of a universal *renovatio* to be brought about by the victory of a social class or even of a political party or personality" (*ibid.*, p. 271).

the Australians, who live by gathering and small-game hunting, is not the same as that of the Neolithic agriculturalists; just as the World of the latter is neither that of the city dwellers of the ancient Near East nor the "World" in which the peoples of Western Europe and the United States live today. The differences are too great to require pointing out. We have mentioned them only to avoid a misunderstanding: in citing examples representing different types of culture, we have no intention of returning to a "confusionistic" comparatism in the manner of Frazer. The historical context of each example we give is implied. But we think it unnecessary, in the case of every tribe cited, to define its social and economic structure and state with what tribes it can or cannot be compared.

The "World," then, is always the world that one knows and in which one lives; it differs from one type of culture to another; hence there are a considerable number of "Worlds." But what is significant for our study is the fact that, despite the differences in their socioeconomic structure and the variety of their cultural contexts, the archaic peoples believe that the World must be annually renewed and that this renewal is brought about by following a model—the cosmogony, or an origin myth that plays the role of a cosmogonic myth.

Obviously, the "Year" is variously conceived by primitives, and the dates of the "New Year" differ in accordance with climate, geographical setting, type of culture, and so on. But there is always a cycle, that is, a period of time that has a beginning and an end. Now, the end of one cycle and the beginning of the next are marked by a series of rituals whose purpose is the renewal of the World. As we said, this *renovatio* is a re-creation after the model of the cosmogony.

The simplest examples are found among the Australians. They are origin myths that are re-enacted annually. The animals and plants created *in illo tempore* by the Supernatural Beings are ritually re-created. In Kimberley the rock paintings, which are believed to have been painted by the Ancestors, are repainted in order to reactivate their creative force, as it was first manifested in mythical times, that is, at the beginning of the World.[5]

For the Australians, this re-creation of food animals and food plants is equivalent to re-creating the World. And this is so not only because, with a sufficient food supply, they hope to live through another year, but above all because the World really came to birth when the animals and plants first made their appearance in the Dream Times. Animals and plants are among the creative works accomplished by the Supernatural Beings. Feeding oneself is not merely a physiological act but is equally a "religious" act; one eats the creations of the Supernatural Beings, and one eats them as they were eaten by the mythical ancestors for the first time, at the beginning of the World.[6]

Among the Australians the cosmogony is limited to the creation of the territory with which they are familiar. This is their "World," and it must be periodically renewed or it may perish. The idea that the Cosmos is threatened with ruin if it is not annually re-created provides the inspiration for the chief festival of the Californian Karok, Hupa, and Yurok tribes. In the respective languages the ceremony is called

[5] Helmut Petri, *Sterbende Welt in Nordwest Australien* (Braunschweig, 1954), pp. 200 ff.; A. P. Elkin, *The Australian Aborigines* (London, 1954), pp. 220 ff.

[6] On the religious value of food, cf. Eliade, "Dimensions religieuses du renouvellement cosmique," p. 273.

"repair" or "fixing" of the world, and, in English, "New Year." Its purpose is to re-establish or strengthen the Earth for the following year or two years. Among some Yurok tribes the strengthening of the World is accomplished by ritually rebuilding the steam cabin, a rite that is cosmogonic in structure and of which other examples will be given later. The essential part of the ceremonial consists in long pilgrimages undertaken by the priest to all the sacred sites, that is, to the places where the Immortals performed certain acts. These ritual peregrinations continue for ten or twelve days. During all this time the priest incarnates the Immortals. As he walks, he thinks: "The ixkareya animas (i.e., one of the Immortals) walked over this in mythical times." When he comes to one of the sacred sites he begins to sweep it, saying: "Ixkareya yakam is sweeping this time, sweeping all the sickness out of this world." Afterward he climbs a mountain. There he finds a branch, which he makes into a walking stick, saying: "This world is cracked, but when I pick up and drag the stick, all the cracks will fill up and the earth will become solid again." Going down to the river, he finds a stone, which he sets solidly in place, saying: "The earth, which has been tipped, will be straight again. People will live to be stronger." He sits down on the stone. "When I sit on the stone," he explained to Gifford, "the earth will never get up and tip again." The stone has been there since the time of the Immortals, that is, since the beginning of the World.[7]

"Taken together, the rituals we have reviewed make up a cosmogonic scenario. In mythical Times, the Immortals

---

[7] A. L. Kroeber and E. W. Gifford, *World Renewal, a Cult System of Native Northwest California,* Anthropological Records, vol. XIII, No. I (University of California, Berkeley, 1949), pp. 6 ff., 14–17, 19 ff., summarized in "Dimensions religieuses du renouvellement cosmique," pp. 259 ff.

created the World in which the California Indians were to live: they traced its outlines, established its Center and its foundations, ensured an abundant supply of salmon and acorns, and exorcised sicknesses. But this World is no longer the atemporal and unchangeable Cosmos in which the Immortals dwelt. It is a living world—inhabited and used by creatures of flesh and blood, subject to the law of becoming, of old age and death. Hence it requires a periodical repairing, a renewing, a strengthening. But the only way to renew the World is to repeat what the Immortals did *in illo tempore,* is to reiterate the creation. This is why the priest reproduces the exemplary itinerary of the Immortals and repeats their acts and words. In short, the priest ends by incarnating the Immortals. In other words, at the time of the New Year the Immortals are believed to be present on earth once again. This explains why the ritual of annually renewing the World is the most important religious ceremony among these California tribes. The World is not only made more stable and regenerated, it is also sanctified by the symbolic presence of the Immortals. The priest, who incarnates them, becomes— for a certain length of time—an 'immortal person,' and, as such, he must be neither looked at nor touched. He performs the rites far from other men, in absolute solitude, for when the Immortals performed them for the first time there were yet no men on earth."[8]

Differences and similarities

The mythico-ritual scenario of periodic renewal of the World is also found among other Californian tribes—for ex-

[8] Eliade, "Dimensions religieuses . . ." pp. 261–262.

ample, the *aki* ceremony of the Hill Maidu, the *hesi* of the Plains Maidu, the *kuksu* of the Eastern Pomo.[9] In all these examples the renewal of the World forms part of a cult complex that includes honoring the Supreme Being, ensuring a good harvest, and the initiation of youths. This Californian scenario may be compared with the Shawnee ritual "The Cabin of New Life" (which forms part of the Sun Dance) and the "Big House" ceremonies of the Lenape. In both cases we find a cosmogonic ritual, a renewal of the World and rebirth of Life. Among the Shawnee the priest renews Creation; among the Lenape the New Year's ceremony reiterates the first creation of the World, to the end of recovering the fullness of the beginnings.[10]

We may add that the building or periodic repairing of the ritual cabin also has a cosmogonic meaning. The sacred cabin represents the Universe. Its roof symbolizes the vault of heaven, the floor the Earth, the four walls the four directions of cosmic space. The Dakotas say: the "Year is a circle around the World," that is, around the initiation cabin.[11] We may also add that the interdependence between the Cosmos and cosmic Time ("circular" Time) was so strongly felt that in several languages the term for "World" is also used to mean "Year." For example. certain California tribes say "The world is past," or "The earth is passed," to mean that "a year has passed."[12]

If we now turn to the New Year rituals that obtain among

[9] Werner Müller, *Weltbild und Kult der Kwakiutl-Indianer* (Wiesbaden, 1955), p. 120.

[10] Werner Müller, *Die Religionen der Waldlandindianer Nordamerikas* (Berlin, 1956), pp. 306, 317.

[11] Werner Müller, *Die blaue Hütte. Zum Sinnbild der Perle bei nordamerikanischen Indianern* (Wiesbaden, 1954), p. 133.

[12] A. L. Kroeber, *Handbook of the Indians of California* (Washington, 1925), pp. 177, 498.

peoples practicing protoagriculture (i.e., cultivation of tubers) we are struck by the differences. We first note two new elements: the collective return of the dead and orgiastic excesses. But the outstanding difference is in religious atmosphere. Instead of the Karok priest's solitary pilgrimage, meditations, and prayers, we find a collective festival of the highest intensity. We need only think of the *milamala* festival of the Trobrianders, described by Malinowski. V. Lanternari has devoted a whole book to a study of this mythico-ritual complex, and we, too, have discussed it briefly in connection with the Melanesian prophetic cults.[13] There is no need to give all the results of these studies here. We will only say that, despite the differences between the mythico-ritual systems of the North American tribes cited above and those of the Melanesians, the structures of the two systems can be homologized. In both cases the Cosmos must be periodically recreated and the cosmogonic scenario through which the renewal is accomplished is related to the new harvest and the sacramentalization of food.

New Year and cosmogony in the ancient Near East

It is significant that similar ideas are found in the religions of the ancient Near East, though of course with the inevitable differences between societies in the pre- and protoagricultural stage and fully agricultural and urban societies, such as Mesopotamia and Egypt. Yet one fact—and it seems to us an essential fact—remains. The Egyptians, the Mesopotamians, the Jews, and other peoples of the ancient Near East felt the

[13] Vittorio Lanternari, *La Grande Festa* (Milan, 1959); M. Eliade, "Dimensions religieuses du renouvellement cosmique," pp. 243 ff.

need to renew the World periodically. The renewal consisted in a cult scenario the chief rite of which symbolized the reiteration of the cosmogony. The facts and their interpretation will be found in the copious specialized literature on the subject[14] and in one chapter of *The Myth of the Eternal Return* (pp. 51 ff.). However, we will repeat that in Mesopotamia the Creation of the World was ritually reiterated during the New Year festival (*akītu.*) A series of rites re-enacted the fight between Marduk and Tiamat (the Dragon symbolizing the primordial Ocean), the victory of the God, and his cosmogonic labors. The "Poem of Creation" (*Enuma elish*) was recited in the Temple. As H. Frankfort puts it, "each New Year shared something essential with the first day when the world was created and the cycle of the seasons started."[15] But examining the New Year rites more closely, we realize that the Mesopotamians felt that the *beginning* was organically connected with an *end* that preceded it, that this "end" was of the same nature as the "Chaos" preceding Creation, and that hence the end was indispensable for every new beginning.

As we mentioned above, among the Egyptains too the New Year symbolized the Creation. As to the Jewish New Year scenario, Mowinckel writes that "one of the chief ideas was the enthronement of Yahweh as king of the world, the symbolic representation of His victory over His enemies, both the forces of chaos and the historical enemies of Israel. The result of this victory was the renewal of creation, election, and the covenant, ideas and rites from the old fertility festivals

[14] Cf. some bibliographical references in *The Myth of the Eternal Return,* p. 57, n. 7.
[15] H. Frankfort, *op. cit.,* p. 319.

which lay behind the historical festival."[16] Later, in the eschatology of the prophets, the restoration of Israel by Yahweh was taken to be a New Creation that implied a sort of return to Paradise.[17]

Obviously, the symbolic reiterations of the cosmogony at the New Year in Mesopotamia and in Israel cannot be put on the same plane. Among the Jews the archaic scenario of the periodic renewal of the World was progressively historicized, while still preserving something of its original meaning. Wensinck had shown that the New Year ritual scenario, which signified the passage from Chaos to Cosmos, was applied to such historical events as the exodus and the crossing of the Red Sea, the conquest of Canaan, the Babylonian captivity and the return from exile, etc.[18] Von Rad, for his part, proved that a single historical event, such as "the constitution of Israel at Mount Sinai through Yahweh and his servant Moses, when it becomes effective in the order of the people, does not have to remain in the sphere of remembrance through oral tradition or written narrative, but can be submitted to ritual renewal in a cult in the same manner as the cosmological order of the neighboring empires."[19] Eric Voegelin rightly stresses the fact that "the symbolic forms of the cosmological empires and of Israel are not mutually exclusive. . . . The ritual renewal of order, one of the symbolic elements developed within the cosmological civilizations, for instance,

[16] S. Mowinckel, *He That Cometh,* trans. by G. W. Anderson (New York, 1956), p. 26.

[17] *Ibid.,* p. 144.

[18] A. J. Wensinck, "The Semitic New Year and the Origin of Eschatology," *Acta Orientalia,* vol. I (1923), pp. 159–199.

[19] Von Rad, summarized in Eric Voegelin, *Order and History, I: Israel and Revelation* (Louisiana State University Press, 1956), p. 294.

runs through the history of mankind from the Babylonian
New Year festival, through Josiah's renewal of the Berith and
the sacramental renewal of Christ, to Machiavelli's *ritornar
ai principij*, because the fall from the order of being, and the
return to it, is a fundamental problem in human existence."[20]

The "perfection of the beginnings"

Hence, however great the differences between the Mesopotamian and Jewish cult systems, they still obviously share
a common hope for the annual or periodic regeneration of
the World. In general, there is a belief in the possibility of
recovering the absolute "beginning"—which implies the symbolic destruction and abolition of the old world. Hence the
end is implied in the beginning and vice versa. There is
nothing surprising in this, for the exemplary image of this
beginning preceded and followed by an end is the Year,
circular cosmic Time, as it can be perceived in the rhythm of
the seasons and the regularity of celestial phenomena.

But here a distinction must be made. If it is probable that
the intuition of the "Year" as a cycle is at the bottom of the
idea of a Cosmos that periodically renews itself, in the mythico-
ritual New Year scenarios[21] another idea, an idea different
in origin and structure, is discernible. It is the idea of the
"perfection of the beginnings," the expression of a more intimate and deeper religious experience, nourished by the imaginary memory of a "Lost Paradise," of a state of bliss that
preceded the present human condition. It is possible that the
mythico-ritual New Year scenario has played such an im-

[20] *Ibid.*, p. 299.
[21] As also, be it added, in countless other cosmogonic and origin myths.

portant role in the history of humanity principally because, by ensuring renewal of the Cosmos, it also offered the hope that the bliss of the "beginnings" could be recovered. The image of the "Year-Circle" became charged with an ambivalent cosmico-vital symbolism, at once "optimistic" and "pessimistic." For the flux of Time implies an ever greater distance from the "beginnings," and hence loss of the original perfection. Whatever endures wastes away, degenerates, and finally perishes. Obviously, we here have a "vitalistic" expression of Reality; but it must not be forgotten that, for the primitive, being reveals itself—and expresses itself—in terms of life. Fullness and force are at the beginning; this is what we might call the "pessimism" inherent in the conception. But we must immediately add: fullness, though very quickly lost, is periodically recoverable. The Year has an end, that is to say, it is automatically followed by a new beginning.

The idea that perfection was at the beginning appears to be quite old. In any case, it is extremely widespread. Then too, it is an idea capable of being indefinitely reinterpreted and incorporated into an endless variety of religious conceptions. We shall have occasion to discuss some of these valuations. We may say at once that the idea of the perfection of the beginnings played an important role in the systematic elaboration of ever more embracing cosmic cycles. The ordinary "Year" was vastly extended by producing a "great Year" or cosmic cycle of incalculable duration. In proportion as the cosmic cycle became longer, the idea of the perfection of the beginnings tended to imply a complementary idea: that, *for something genuinely new to begin, the vestiges and ruins of the old cycle must be completely destroyed*. In other words, to obtain an *absolute* beginning, the end of a World must be total. Eschatology is only the prefiguration of a cosmogony to come. But every eschatology insists on this fact: the New Creation cannot take place before this world is abolished once and for all. There is no question of regenerating what has degenerated; nothing will serve but to destroy the old world so that it can be re-created *in toto*. The obsession with the bliss of the beginnings demands the destruction of all that has existed—and hence has degenerated —since the beginning of the World; there is no other way to restore the initial perfection.

To be sure, all these nostalgias and beliefs are already present in the mythico-ritual scenarios of the annual renewal of the World. But from the protoagricultural stage of culture on, there was a growing acceptance of the idea that there are also *real* (not merely ritual) destructions and re-creations of the World, that there is a "return to the origin" in the literal sense, that is, a relapse of the Cosmos to the amorphous, chaotic state, followed by a new cosmogony.

This conception is best illustrated by the myths of the End of the World. We shall study them in the next chapter—not only for their intrinsic interest, but also because they can cast light on the function of myths in general. Until now we have dealt only with cosmogonic and origin myths, with myths telling *what has already taken place*. It is now time to see how the idea of the "perfection of the beginnings" was also projected into a timeless future. The myths of the End of the World have certainly played an important role in the history of mankind. They have shown that the "origin" is "movable." For, after a certain moment, the "origin" is no longer found only in a mythical past but also in a fabulous future. This, of course, is the conclusion that the Stoics and Neo-Pythagoreans reached by systematically elaborating the idea of "eternal return." But the notion of the "origin" is primarily bound up with the idea of perfection and bliss. So it is in conceptions of eschatology understood as a cosmogony of the future that we find the sources of all beliefs that proclaim the Age of Gold to be not merely (or no longer) in the past but also (or only) in the future.

IV.

Eschatology and Cosmogony

The End of the World—in the past and the future

IN SUMMARY form, it could be said that, for primitives, the End of the World has already occurred, although it is to be repeated in a more or less distant future. Myths of cosmic cataclysms are extremely widespread. They tell how the World was destroyed and mankind annihilated except for a single couple or a few survivors. The myths of the Flood are the most numerous and are known nearly everywhere (although extremely infrequent in Africa).[1] In addition to Flood myths, others recount the destruction of mankind by cataclysms of cosmic proportions—earthquakes, conflagrations, falling mountains, epidemics, and so forth. Clearly, this End of the World was not final; rather, it was the end of one human race, followed by the appearance of another. But the total submergence of the Earth under the Waters or its destruction by fire, followed by the emergence of a virgin Earth, symbolize return to Chaos followed by cosmogony.

In many myths the Flood is connected with a ritual fault

---

[1] Cf. Sir James George Frazer, *Folk-Lore in the Old Testament* (London, 1919), vol. I, pp. 329–332; Clyde Kluckhohn, "Recurrent Themes in Myths and Mythmaking," *Daedalus* Spring 1959 p. 271. The essential bibliography on legends of the Flood is to be found in Stith Thompson, *Motif-Index of Folk-Literature* (new ed., Bloomington, Ind., 1955), vol. I, p. 184 (A 1010).

that aroused the wrath of the Supreme Being; sometimes it is merely the result of a Divine Being's wish to put an end to humanity. But if we examine the myths that announce the impending Flood, we find that one of its chief causes is the sins of mankind together with the decrepitude of the World. The Flood opened the way at once to a re-creation of the World and to a regeneration of humanity. In other words, the End of the World in the past and that which is to take place in the future both represent the mythico-ritual system of the New Year festival projected on the macrocosmic scale and given an unusual degree of intensity. But now we no longer have what might be called the "natural end" of the World ("natural" because it coincides with the end of the Year and hence forms an integral part of the cosmic cycle); there is a *real* catastrophe, brought on by Divine Beings. The symmetry between the Flood and the annual renewal of the World was realized in some very few cases (Mesopotamia, Judaism, Mandan).[2] But in general the Flood myths are independent from the mythico-ritual New Year scenarios. This is easy to understand, for the periodic festivals of regeneration symbolically re-enact the cosmogony, the creative work of the Gods, not the destruction of the old world; the latter disappeared "naturally" for the simple reason that the distance that separated it from the "beginnings" had reached its extreme limit.

In comparison with myths describing the End of the World in the past, myths referring to an end to come are curiously scarce among primitives. As F. R. Lehmann[3] remarks, their scarcity is perhaps due to the fact that ethnologists did not

[2] Cf. Eliade, *Myth of the Eternal Return,* pp. 57–58, 59, 72, n. 41.
[3] F. R. Lehmann, "Weltunterganag und Welterneuerung im Glauben schriftloser Völker," *Zeitschrift für Ethnologie,* vol. LXXI (1931), p. 103.

ask this particular question in their investigations. It is sometimes difficult to determine whether the myth concerns a past
catastrophe or one to come. According to E. H. Man, the
Andamanese believe that after the End of the World a new
humanity, enjoying a paradisal condition, will appear; there
will be no more sickness or old age or death. After the catastrophe the dead will rise again. But according to A. Radcliffe
Brown, Man seems to have combined a number of versions
collected from different informants. Actually, Brown goes on,
the myth does relate the End and the re-creation of the World;
but it applies to the past, not to the future. But since, as
Lehmann observes, the Andamanese language has no future
tense,[4] it is not easy to be sure whether an event is in the
past or in the future.

The scarcest among primitive myths of the End are those
which say nothing definite about a possible re-creation of the
World. Thus the Kai of New Guinea believe that the Creator,
Mālengfung, after creating the Cosmos and man, withdrew
to the farthest reaches of the World, at the horizon, and there
fell asleep. Whenever he turns over in his sleep the Earth
shakes. But one day he will rise from his bed and destroy
the sky, which will fall in ruins on the Earth and put an end
to all life.[5] In one of the Caroline Islands, Namolut, the
belief has been recorded that the Creator will one day destroy
mankind for its sins. But the Gods will continue to exist—
which implies the possibility of a new creation.[6] In another
of the Carolines, Aurepik, it is the Creator's son who is responsible for the catastrophe. When he sees that the chief

---

[4] *Ibid.,* p. 112.

[5] Richard Thurnwald, *Die Eingeborenen Australiens und der Südseeinseln* (Tübingen, 1927), pp. 26–27, after C. Keysser, *Aus dem Leben der
Kaileute* (in Neuhauss, *Deutsch-Neu-Guinea* [1911], pp. 154 ff.).

[6] F. R. Lehmann, *op. cit.,* p. 107.

of an island no longer feels any concern for his subjects he will submerge the island by a cyclone.[7] Here again it is not clear if the End is final; the idea of a punishment of "sins" usually implies the subsequent creation of a new humanity.

More difficult to interpret are the beliefs of the Negritos of the Malaya Peninsula. They know that one day Karei will put an end to the World because men no longer follow his precepts. So when there is a storm the Negritos try to forestall the catastrophe by expiatory offerings of blood.[8] The catastrophe will be universal, making no distinction between sinners and nonsinners, and apparently will not usher in a New Creation. This is why the Negritos call Karei "evil," and the Ple-Sakai see him as the enemy who "stole Paradise" from them.[9]

A particularly striking example is that of the Guarani of the Matto Grosso. Knowing that the Earth would be destroyed by fire and water, they set out in search of the "Land without Sin," a kind of Earthly Paradise lying beyond the Ocean. These long journeys, prompted by the shamans and made under their guidance, began in the nineteenth century and continued down to 1912. Some tribes believed that the catastrophe would be followed by a renewal of the World and the return of the dead. Other tribes not only expected but actually hoped for the final End of the World.[10] Nimuendaju wrote in 1912: "Not only the Guarani but all the Nature is old and weary of life. How often the medicine-men, when they went to meet, in dream, Nanderuvuvu, have heard the Earth im-

[7] *Ibid.*, p. 117.

[8] Cf. M. Eliade, *Patterns in Comparative Religion* (New York, 1958), pp. 46 ff.

[9] F. R. Lehmann, *op. cit.*, p. 107.

[10] Cf. E. Schader, "Der Paradiesmythos im Leben der Guarani-Indianer," *Staden-Jahrbuch* (São Paulo, 1955), vol. III, pp. 151 ff.; Wilhelm

ploring him: 'I have already devoured too many corpses, I am filled from it, and I am exhausted. Do make an end of it, my Father!' The water also beseeches the Creator to let it rest, disturbed no longer, and so the trees . . . and so all the rest of Nature."[11]

It would be hard to find a more moving expression of cosmic weariness, of the desire for absolute rest and death. But what really lies behind it is the inevitable disenchantment that follows a long and fruitless messianic exaltation. For a century the Guarani looked for the Earthly Paradise, singing and dancing. They had re-evaluated the myth of the End of the World and incorporated it into a millennialist mythology.[12]

Most American myths of the End imply either a cyclic theory (as among the Aztecs), or the belief that the catastrophe will be followed by a new Creation, or, finally (in some parts of North America), the belief in a universal regeneration accomplished without a cataclysm. (In this process of regeneration, only sinners will perish.) According to Aztec tradition, there have already been three or four destructions of the World, and the fourth (or the fifth) is expected in the future. Each of these Worlds is ruled by a "Sun," whose fall or disappearance marks the End.[13]

Koppers, "Prophetismus und Messianismus als völkerkundliches und universalgeschichtliches Problem," *Saeculum,* vol. X (1959), pp. 42 ff.; Robert H. Lowie, "Primitive Messianism and an Ethnological Problem," *Diogenes,* No. 19 (Fall 1957), pp. 70 ff.

[11] Curt Nimuendaju, "Die Sagen von der Erschaffung und Vernichtung der Welt als Grundlagen der Religion der Apapocuva-Guarani," *Zeitschrift für Ethnologie,* vol. XLVI (1914), p. 335.

[12] Cf. R. H. Lowie, *op. cit.,* p. 71.

[13] Cf. H. B. Alexander, *Latin-American Mythology (Mythology of All Races* [Boston, 1920], vol. XI), pp. 91 ff.

We cannot here enumerate all the other important North and South American myths concerning the End of the World. Some of them tell of a couple who will repeople the new World.[14] Thus the Choctaw believe that the World will be destroyed by fire, but men's spirits will return, their bones will be reclothed with flesh, and the risen will again inhabit their ancient lands.[15] A similar myth is found among the Eskimos: men will be reborn from their bones (a belief peculiar to hunting cultures).[16] The belief that the catastrophe is the inevitable consequence of the "old age" or decrepitude of the World appears to be comparatively common. According to the Cherokee, "when the world grows old and worn out, the people will die and the cords will break and let the earth sink down into the Ocean." (The Earth is imagined as a great island suspended from the sky by four cords.)[17] In a Maidu myth Earth-Maker assures the couple he had created: "When this world becomes bad, I will make it over again; and after I make it, ye shall be born."[18] One of the chief cosmogonic myths among the Kato, an Athapascan tribe, begins with the creation of a new sky to replace the old one, which seems

[14] Algonkin myth in Daniel G. Brinton, *The Myths of the New World* (2nd ed. rev., New York, 1876), pp. 235–236. Wintu myth in H. B. Alexander, *North American Mythology* (*Mythology of All Races* [Boston, 1916], vol. X), pp. 223 ff.

[15] Adam Hodgson, *Travels in North America,* p. 280; Brinton, *op. cit.,* pp. 279–280.

[16] Brinton, *op. cit.,* p. 280: He above shall breathe once upon the bones of men, twice upon the bones of women, and they shall come back to life. Another version of the myth was published by Franz Boas, *The Central Eskimo* (GRBEW, 1888), pp. 588 ff. Cf. M. Eliade, *Le Chamanisme et les techniques archaïques de l'extase* (Paris, 1951), pp. 153 ff.

[17] H. B. Alexander, *North American Mythology,* p. 60.

[18] *Ibid.,* p. 219; cf. *ibid.,* pp. 299–300, bibliography on the North American myth of the Flood.

about to fall.[19] As Alexander remarks in connection with the cosmogonic myths of the Pacific coast, "many of the creation-stories seem to be, in fact, traditions of the re-forming of the earth after the great annihilation, although in some myths both the creation and the re-creation are described."[20]

All in all, these myths of the End of the World implying, as they do in clearer or darker fashion, the re-creation of a new Universe, express the same archaic and extremely wide-spread idea of the progressive "degradation" of a Cosmos, necessitating its periodical destruction and re-creation. These myths of a final catastrophe that will at the same time be the sign announcing the imminent re-creation of the World have been the seed bed for the prophetic and millennialist move-ments that have developed among primitive peoples in our day. We shall return to these primitive millennialisms, for, together with Marxist chiliasm, they represent the only posi-tive modern re-evaluations of the End of the World myth. But we must first briefly describe the place which that myth has held in more complex religions.

The End of the World in Oriental religions

In all probability the doctrine of the destruction of the World (*pralaya*) was already known in Vedic times (cf. *Atharva Veda*, X, 8, 39–40). The universal conflagration (*ragnarök*), followed by a new Creation, is an element in

[19] *Ibid.,* p. 222.
[20] *Ibid,* p. 225. On the South American myths concerning the End of the World by fire or by water, cf. P. Ehrenreich, *Die Mythen und Legen-den der Südamerikanen Urvölker* (Berlin, 1905), pp. 30–31. On the South American traditions concerning the renewal of the World after the catastrophe, cf. Claude Lévi-Strauss, in *Bulletin of the Bureau of Amer-ican Ethnology,* vol. CXLIII, no. 3, pp. 347 (Bakairi), 369 (Namicura).

Germanic mythology. These facts seem to show that the Indo-Europeans were not unacquainted with the End of the World myth. Stig Wikander has recently demonstrated the existence of a Germanic myth of the eschatological battle, which has the closest similarities to the parallel Indian and Iranian accounts. But beginning with the Brāhmanas,[21] and especially in the Purānas, the Indians sedulously developed the doctrine of the four *yugas*, the four Ages of the World. The essence of this theory is the cyclical creation and destruction of the World and the belief in the "perfection of the beginnings." As the Buddhists and the Jainas hold the same views, we may conclude that the doctrine of the eternal creation and destruction of the Universe is a pan-Indian idea.

Since we have already discussed the problem in *The Myth of the Eternal Return*, we will not enter into it here. We will only mention some important details. "The complete cycle is terminated by a dissolution, a *pralaya*, which is repeated more intensely (*mahapralaya*, great dissolution) at the end of the thousandth cycle."[22] According to the Mahābharata and the Purānas,[23] the horizon will burst into flame, seven or twelve suns will appear in the heavens and will dry up the seas and burn the Earth. The Samvartaka (the Fire of the Cosmic Conflagration) will destroy the entire Universe. Then rain will fall in floods for twelve years, and the Earth will be submerged and mankind destroyed (Visnu Purāna 24, 25). Sitting on the cosmic snake Śesa on the surface of the Ocean,

[21] The names of the four *yugas* first appear in the *Aitareya Brāhmana*, VII, 14.

[22] *The Myth of the Eternal Return*, p. 114. Cf. also *Images and Symbols* (New York, 1961), pp. 62 ff.

[23] Cf. Emil Abegg, *Der Messiasglaube in Indien und Iran* (Berlin, 1928), p. 34, n. 2.

Visnu is sunk in yogic sleep (Visnu Purāna, VI, 4, 1–11).
And then everything will begin over again—*ad infinitum.*

As to the myth of the "perfection of the beginnings," it is
easily recognized in the purity, intelligence, bliss, and longevity
of human life during the *krta yuga,* the First Age. In the
course of the following *yugas* there is a progressive deterioration in man's intelligence and morality as well as in his
bodily stature and longevity. Jainism expresses the perfection of
the beginnings and the subsequent degeneration in extravagant
terms. According to Hemacandra, in the beginning man's
stature was six miles and his life "lasted a krore of *purvas*
(a *purva* = 8,400,000 years)." But at the end of the cycle
his stature barely reaches seven cubits and his life does not
last more than a hundred years (Jacobi, in ERE, I, 202).
The Buddhists too dwell on the immense shortening of human
life—80,000 years and even more ("immeasurable length,"
according to some traditions) at the beginning of the cycle
and only ten years at the end of it.

The Indian doctrine of the Ages of the World, that is, the
eternal creation, deterioration, destruction, and re-creation
of the Universe, is to some extent similar to the primitive conception of the annual renewal of the World, but there are
important differences. In the Indian theory man plays no part
whatever in the periodic re-creation of the World; basically,
man does not want this eternal re-creation, his goal is escape
from the cosmic cycle.[24] Then, too, the Gods themselves seem
not to be actual Creators; they are more the instruments
through which the cosmic process is accomplished. So we see

[24] We have in mind, obviously, the religious and philosophical elite in
search of a "deliverance" from illusion and suffering. But popular Indian
religious feeling accepts and values human existence in the World.

that for India there is no final End of the World properly speaking; there are only periods of varying lengths between the annihilation of one Universe and the appearance of another. The "End" has no meaning except for the human condition; man can halt the process of transmigration in which he is blindly carried along.

The myth of the perfection of the beginnings is clearly documented among the Mesopotamians, the Jews, and the Greeks. According to Babylonian traditions, the eight or ten antediluvian kings reigned between 10,800 and 72,000 years; in contrast the kings of the first postdiluvian dynasties reigned no more than 1,200 years.[25] The Babylonians also knew the myth of a primordial Paradise and had preserved the memory of a series (probably totaling seven) of successive destructions and re-creations of the human race.[26] The Jews held similar ideas—the loss of the original Paradise, the progressive shortening of the span of human life, the Flood that annihilated humanity except for a few privileged individuals. In Egypt the myth of the "perfection of the beginnings" is not attested, but we find the legendary tradition of the fabulous longevity of the kings before Menes.[27]

In Greece there are two different but connected traditions: (1) the theory of the Ages of the World, including the myth of the perfection of the beginnings, (2) the cyclic doctrine. Hesiod is the first to describe the progressive degeneration of humanity during the five ages (*Works,* 109–201). The first, the Age of Gold under the reign of Kronos, was a sort of Para-

---

[25] W. F. Albright, "Primitivism in Ancient Western Asia," in Arthur O. Lovejoy and George Boas, *Primitivism and Related Ideas in Antiquity* (Baltimore, 1935), p. 422.

[26] *Ibid.,* pp. 424, 426.

[27] *Ibid.,* p. 431.

dise: men lived for a long time, never grew old, and their life was like that of the gods. The cyclic theory makes its appearance with Heraclitus (fr. 66 [22 Bywater]), who will later greatly influence the Stoic doctrine of the Eternal Return. We find the two mythical themes—the Ages of the World and the continuous cycle of creations and destructions—already associated in Empedocles. There is no need to discuss the different forms these theories assumed in Greece, especially as the result of Oriental influences. Suffice it to say that the Stoics took over from Heraclitus the idea of the End of the World by fire (*ekpyrosis*) and that Plato (*Tim.* 22, C) already knew, as an alternative, the End by flood. These two cataclysms in a measure determined the rhythm of the Great Year (*magnus annus*). According to a lost work of Aristotle (*Protrepticus*), the two catastrophes occurred at the two solstices—the *conflagratio* at the summer solstice, the *diluvium* at the winter.[28]

Judaeo-Christian apocalypses

Some of these apocalyptic images of the End of the World recur in the Judaeo-Christian eschatological visions. But Judaeo-Christianity makes an innovation of the first importance. The End of the World will occur only once, just as the cosmogony occurred only once. The Cosmos that will reappear after the catastrophe will be the same Cosmos that God created at the beginning of Time, but purified, regen-

[28] The Indian ideas concerning the End of the World by fire and by water are discernible in these cosmic catastrophes. Cf. also B. L. van der Waerden, "Das Grosse Jahr und die ewige Wiederkehr," *Hermes,* vol. 80 (1950), pp. 129 ff.

erated, restored to its original glory. This Earthly Paradise will not be destroyed again, will have no end. Time is no longer the circular Time of the Eternal Return; it has become a linear and irreversible Time. Nor is this all: the eschatology also represents the triumph of a Sacred History. For the End of the World will reveal the religious value of human acts, and men will be judged by their acts. Here there is no longer any cosmic regeneration implying the accompanying regeneration of a collectivity (or of the whole human race). There is a Judgment, a selection: only the chosen will live in eternal bliss. The chosen, the good, will be saved by their loyalty to a Sacred History; faced by the powers and the temptations of this world, they remained true to the Kingdom of Heaven.

Further in distinction from the cosmic religions, for Judaeo-Christianity the End of the World is part of the Messianic mystery. For the Jews the coming of the Messiah will announce the End of the World and the restoration of Paradise. For the Christians the End of the World will precede the second coming of Christ and the Last Judgment. But for both alike the triumph of Sacred History—manifested by the End of the World—in some measure implies the restoration of Paradise. The prophets proclaim that the Cosmos will be renewed—there will be a new Heaven and a new Earth. There will be an abundance of all things, as in the Garden of Eden.[29] Wild beasts will live in peace together and "a little child shall lead them" (Isa. 11:6). Sicknesses and infirmities will vanish forever; the lame will walk, the deaf hear, the dumb speak, the blind see, and there will be no more weeping

[29] Amos 9:13 ff.; Isa. 30:23 ff.; 35:1, 2, 7; 65:17; 66:22; Hos. 1:10; 2:18 ff.; Zech. 8:12; Ezek. 34:14, 27; 36:9 ff., 30, 35.

and tears (Isa. 30:19, 35:3 ff.; Ezek. 34:16). The new
Israel will be built on Mount Zion because Paradise was set
on a mountain (Isa. 35:10; Ps. 48:2). For the Christians,
too, the total renewal of the Cosmos and the restoration of
Paradise are essential characteristics of the *eschaton*. In the
Apocalypse of John (21:1–5) we read: "And I saw a new
heaven and a new earth: for the first heaven and the first
earth were passed away. . . . And I heard a great voice out
of heaven saying . . . : 'and there shall be no more death,
neither sorrow, nor crying, neither shall there be any more
pain. . . . Behold, I make all things new.' "

But this New Creation will rise on the ruins of the first.
The syndrome of the final catastrophe resembles the Indian
descriptions of the destruction of the Universe. There will be
drought and famine, and the days will grow short.[30] The period
immediately preceding the End will be dominated by Antichrist. But Christ will come and will purify the World by
fire. As Ephraim the Syrian expresses it: "The sea shall roar
and be dried up . . . the heaven and earth shall be dissolved,
and darkness and smoke shall prevail. Against the earth shall
the Lord send fire, which lasting 40 days shall cleanse it from
wickedness and the stains of sins."[31] The destroying fire appears only once in the New Testament, in the Second Epistle
of Peter (3:6–14). But it is an important element in the
Sibylline Oracles, in Stoicism, and in later Christian literature.
It is probably Iranian in origin.[32]

The reign of Antichrist is in some sense equivalent to a
return to Chaos. On the one hand, Antichrist is presented

---

[30] W. Bousset, *The Antichrist Legend* (English trans., London, 1896),
pp. 195 ff., 218 ff.

[31] Ephr. Syr., ch. II, quoted in Bousset, p. 238.

[32] Cf. *The Myth of the Eternal Return,* pp. 124 ff.

in the form of a dragon or a demon,[33] and this is reminiscent of the old myth of the fight between God and the Dragon; the fight took place in the beginning, before the Creation of the World, and it will take place again at the End. On the other hand, when Antichrist comes to be regarded as the false Messiah his reign will represent the total overthrow of social, moral, and religious values—in other words, the return to chaos. In the course of the centuries Antichrist was identified with various historical figures, from Nero to the Pope (by Luther). The important fact is that certain particularly tragic historical periods were held to be dominated by Antichrist—but at the same time there was always the hope that his reign announced the imminent coming of Christ. Cosmic catastrophes, scourges, historical terror, the seeming triumph of Evil made up the apocalyptic syndrome[34] which was to precede Christ's return and the millennium.

Christian millennialisms

After becoming the official religion of the Roman Empire, Christianity condemned millennialism as heretical, although illustrious Fathers had professed it in the past. But the Church had accepted History, and the *eschaton* was no longer the imminent event that it had been during the persecutions. The World—this world below, with all its sins, injustices, and cruelties—continued. God alone knew the hour of the End of the World, and one thing seemed certain: the End was

[33] Cf. W. Bousset, *The Antichrist Legend*, pp. 145 ff. Cf. also R. Mayer, *Die biblische Vorstellung vom Weltenbrand* (Bonn, 1957).
[34] See also A. A. Vasiliev, "Medieval Ideas of the End of the World: West and East," *Byzantion* (Boston, 1944), vol. XVI, Fasc. 2, 1942–43, pp. 462–502.

not near. With the triumph of the Church, the Kingdom of Heaven was already present on earth, and in a certain sense the old world had already been destroyed. In this official anti-millennialism of the Church we recognize the first manifestation of the doctrine of progress. The Church had accepted the World as it was, though it sought to make human life a little less wretched than it had been during the great historical crises. The Church had taken this position against the prophets and apocalyptic visionaries of every dye.

Some centuries later, after Islam burst into the Mediterranean, but especially after the eleventh century, millennialist and eschatological movements reappeared—this time aimed against the Church or its hierarchy. These movements have a number of common features. Their inspirers expect and announce the restoration of the Earthly Paradise after a period of terrible trials and cataclysms. Luther, too, expected the imminent End of the World. For centuries the same religious idea recurs again and again: this world—the World of History—is unjust, abominable, demonic; fortunately, it is already decaying, the catastrophes have begun, this old world is cracking everywhere; very soon it will be annihilated, the powers of darkness will be conquered once and for all, the "good" will triumph, Paradise will be regained. All the millennialist and eschatological movements display optimism. They react against the terror of History with an energy that only the extremity of despair can arouse. But for centuries the great Christian orthodoxies had no longer felt the eschatological tension. Expectation of the End of the World and the imminence of the Last Judgment are characteristic of none of the great Christian churches. Millennialism barely survives in some recent Christian sects.

Eschatological and millennialist mythology recently reappeared in Europe in two totalitarian political movements. Although radically secularized in appearance, Nazism and Communism are loaded with eschatological elements: they announce the end of this world and the beginning of an age of plenty and bliss. Norman Cohn, the author of the most recent book on millennialism, writes of National Socialism and Marxism-Leninism: "Beneath the pseudo-scientific terminology one can in each case recognize a phantasy of which almost every element is to be found in phantasies which were already current in medieval Europe. The final, decisive battle of the Elect (be they the 'Aryan race' or the 'proletariat') against the hosts of evil (be they the Jews or the 'bourgeoisie'); a dispensation on which the Elect are to be most amply compensated for all their sufferings by the joys of total domination or of total community or of both together; a world purified of all evil and in which history is to find its consummation—these ancient imaginings are with us still."[35]

Millennialism among "primitives"

But it is more especially outside of the Western orbit that the End of the World myth is flourishing with considerable vigor today. We refer to the countless nativist and millennialist movements, of which the best known are the Melanesian "cargo cults" but which are also found in other parts of Oceania as well as in the former European colonies cf Africa. In all probability most of these movements arose after more or less prolonged contacts with Christianity. Although nearly

[35] Norman Cohn, *The Pursuit of the Millennium* (New York, 1957), p. 308.

all of them are antiwhite and antichristian, the majority of these native millennialisms include Christian eschatological elements. In some cases the natives revolt against the missionaries precisely because the latter do not behave like true Christians and, for example, do not believe in the imminent coming of Christ and the resurrection of the dead. In Melanesia the cargo cults have assimilated the myths and rituals of the New Year. As we saw earlier, the New Year festivals imply the symbolic re-creation of the World. The disciples of the cargo cults likewise believe that the Cosmos will be destroyed and re-created and that the tribe will regain a kind of Paradise—the dead will rise again and there will be neither death nor sickness. But as in the Indo-Iranian and Judaeo-Christian eschatologies, this new creation—or recovery of Paradise—will be preceded by a series of cosmic catastrophes. The earth will shake, there will be rains of fire, the mountains will crumble and fill the valleys, the whites and the natives who have not joined the cult will be annihilated, and so on.

The morphology of primitive millennialisms is extremely rich and complex. For our purpose the important aspects are these: (1) the millennialist movements may be considered a development of the mythico-ritual scenario of the periodic renewal of the World; (2) the influence, direct or indirect, of Christian eschatology almost always seems beyond question; (3) though attracted by Western values and wishing to acquire the religion and education of the whites no less than their wealth and weapons, the adherents of the millennialist movements are always anti-Western; (4) these movements are always begun by strong religious personalities of the prophetic type, and are organized or expanded by politicians for political ends; (5) for all of them the millennium is imminent, but it will not come without cosmic cataclysms or historical catastrophes.[36]

There is no need to dwell on the political, social, and economic character of these movements—it is sufficiently obvious. But their strength, their influence, and their creativity do not reside solely in these socio-economic factors. They are religious movements. Their disciples expect and announce the End of the World in order to achieve a better economic and social condition—but above all because they hope for a re-creation of the World and a restoration of human happiness. They hunger and thirst after worldly goods—but also for the immortality, the freedom, and the bliss of Paradise. For them the End of the World is the condition for establishing a form of human life that will be blissful, perfect, and eternal.

We should add that even where there is no question of a catastrophic end, the idea of regeneration, of a re-creation of the World, is the essential element of the movement. The prophet or founder of the cult proclaims the imminent "return to the origins," and hence the recovery of the first, "paradisal," state. To be sure, in many cases this "original" paradisal state represents the idealized image of the cultural and economic situation before the coming of the whites. This is not the only example of the "original state," a people's "ancient history," being mythicized as an Age of Gold. But what is to our purpose is not the "historical" reality that can sometimes be abstracted and isolated from this exuberant flowering of images, but the fact that the End of a World—the world of colonization—and the expectation of a New

---

[36] Cf. M. Eliade, "Dimensions religieuses du renouvellement cosmique," *Eranos-Jahrbuch* (Zurich, 1960), vol. XXVIII.

World imply a return to origins. The messianic figure is identified with the Culture Hero or the mythical Ancestor whose return was awaited. Their coming is equivalent to a reinstallation of the mythical Times of the origin, hence to a recreation of the World. The political independence and the cultural freedom proclaimed by the millennialist movements among the colonial peoples are conceived as the recovery of an original state of bliss. In short, even without a *visible* apocalyptic destruction, this world, the old world, is symbolically abolished and the paradisal World of the origin is established in its place.

The "End of the World" in modern art

Western societies have nothing comparable to the optimism shown by Communist eschatology and the primitive millennialisms. On the contrary, today there is an ever more intense fear of a catastrophic End of the World brought about by thermonuclear weapons. In the thought of the West this End will be total and final; it will not be followed by a new Creation of the World. We cannot here undertake a systematic analysis of the many and various expressions of atomic fear in the modern world. But other Western cultural phenomena seem to us significant for our investigation. Since the beginning of the century the plastic arts, as well as literature and music, have undergone such radical transformations that it has been possible to speak of a "destruction of the language of art." Beginning in painting, this destruction of language has spread to poetry, to the novel, and just recently, with Ionesco, to the theater. In some cases there is a real annihilation of the established artistic Universe. Looking at some recent canvases, we get the impression that the artist wished to make *tabula rasa* of the entire history of painting. There is more than a destruction, there is a reversion to Chaos, to a sort of primordial *massa confusa*. Yet at the same time, contemplating such works, we sense that the artist is searching for something that he has not yet expressed. He had to make a clean sweep of the ruins and trash accumulated by the preceding plastic revolutions; he had to reach a germinal mode of matter, so that he could begin the history of art over again from zero. Among many modern artists we sense that the "destruction of the plastic language" is only the first phase of a more complex process and that the re-creation of a new Universe must necessarily follow.

In modern art the nihilism and pessimism of the first revolutionaries and demolishers represent attitudes that are already outmoded. Today no great artist believes in the degeneration and imminent disappearance of his art. From this point of view the modern artists' attitude is like that of the "primitives"; they have contributed to the destruction of the World—that is, to the destruction of *their* World, their artistic Universe—in order to create another. But this cultural phenomenon is of the utmost importance, for it is primarily the artists who represent the genuine creative forces of a civilization or a society. Through their creation the artists anticipate what is to come—sometimes one or two generations later—in other sectors of social and cultural life.

It is significant that the destruction of artistic languages has coincided with the rise of psychoanalysis. Depth psychology has given currency to the interest in origins, an interest that is so typical of the man of the archaic societies. It would be intensely interesting to study the process of re-evaluation undergone by the myth of the End of the World in contemporary art. We should see that artists, far from being the neurotics the are often said to be, are, on the contrary, more healthy psychically than many modern men. They have understood that a true new beginning can come only after a real End. And, the first among moderns, the artists have set themselves to destroying *their* World in order to re-create an artistic Universe in which man can at once live and contemplate and dream.

V.

Time Can Be Overcome

Certainty of a new beginning

OUR BRIEF considerations on the similarity between the "optimism" of the recently decolonialized peoples and that of modern Western artists could have been carried further and developed. For other comparisons between certain beliefs of traditional societies and certain aspects of modern culture spring to mind. But we shall defer these comparisons until later, in order not to interrupt our exposition. For if we examined the mythical theme of the End of the World, it was primarily to bring out the relations between eschatology and cosmogony. The reader will remember that in the third chapter we emphasized the extreme importance of the mythico-ritual scenario of annual World regeneration. We saw there that this scenario implies the motif of the "perfection of the beginnings" and that, after a certain historical moment, this motif becomes "movable"; it can now signify not only the perfection of the beginnings in the mythical past but also the perfection that is to come in the future, after this World is destroyed.

In our long excursus on the End-of-the-World myths analyzed in the preceding chapter, we sought to make it clear that, even in eschatologies, the essential thing is not the fact

of the *End,* but the certainty of a *new beginning.* Now, this
rebeginning is, properly speaking, the counterpart to the absolute beginning, the cosmogony. It could be said that here,
too, we have found the mental attitude typical of archaic man:
the exceptional value he attributes to *knowledge of origins.*
For the man of the archaic societies, that is, knowledge of
the origin of each thing (animal, plant, cosmic object, etc.)
confers a kind of magical mastery over it; he knows where
to find it and how to make it reappear in the future. The
same formula could be applied to the eschatological myths:
knowledge of what took place *ab origine,* of the cosmogony,
gives knowledge of what will come to pass in the future.
The "movability" of the origin of the World expresses man's
hope that his World *will always be there,* even if it is periodically destroyed in the strict sense of the word. Is this a desperate solution? No—because the idea of the destruction of
the World is not, basically, pessimistic. Through its own
duration the World degenerates and wears out; this is why
it must be symbolically re-created every year. But it was possible to accept the idea of the apocalyptic destruction of the
World because the cosmogony—that is, the "secret" of the
origin of the World—was known.

Freud and knowledge of the "origin"

There is no need to dwell further on the "existential"
value of knowledge of the origin in the traditional societies.
This type of behavior is not exclusively archaic. The desire
to know the origin of things is also characteristic of Western
culture. The eighteenth century, and especially the nineteenth,
saw a multiplication of disciplines investigating not only the

origin of the Universe, of life, of the species, or of man, but also the origin of society, language, religion, and all human institutions. The goal was to discover the origin and history of everything that surrounds us—the origin of the solar system and, no less, the origin of an institution such as marriage or of a children's game such as hopscotch.

In the twentieth century the scientific study of beginnings took a different direction. For psychoanalysis, for example, the truly primordial is the "human primordial," earliest childhood. The child lives in a mythical, paradisal time.[1] Psychoanalysis developed techniques capable of showing us the "beginnings" of our personal history, and especially of identifying the particular event that put an end to the bliss of childhood and determined the future orientation of our life. "Restating this in terms of archaic thinking, one might say that there was once a 'paradise' (which for psychoanalysis is the prenatal period, or the time before weaning), ending with a 'break' or 'catastrophe' (the infantile trauma), and that whatever the adult's attitude may be toward these primordial circumstances, they are none the less constitutive of his being."[2]

It is of interest to note that, of all the vital sciences, only psychoanalysis arrives at the idea that the "beginnings" of every human being are blissful and constitute a sort of Para-

---

[1] This is why the unconscious displays the structure of a private mythology. We can go even further and say not only that the unconscious is "mythological" but also that some of its contents carry cosmic values; in other words, that they reflect the modalities, processes, and destiny of life and living matter. It can even be said that modern man's only real contact with cosmic sacrality is effected by the unconscious, whether in his dreams and his imaginative life or in the creations that arise out of the unconscious (poetry, games, spectacles, etc.).

[2] M. Eliade, *Myths, Dreams and Mysteries,* p. 54.

dise, whereas the other vital sciences stress especially the precariousness and imperfection of the beginnings. For them, it is process, becoming, evolution that gradually corrects the difficulty and poverty of the "beginnings."

Two of Freud's ideas are relevant to our subject: (1) the bliss of the "origin" and "beginnings" of the human being, and (2) the idea that through memory, or by a "going back," one can relive certain traumatic incidents of early childhood. The bliss of the "origin" is, we have seen, a quite frequent theme in the archaic religions; it is attested in India, Iran, Greece, and in Judaeo-Christianity. The fact that Freud postulates bliss at the beginning of human existence does not mean that psychoanalysis has a mythological structure or that it borrows an archaic mythical theme or accepts the Judaeo-Christian myth of Paradise and Fall. The only connection that can be made between psychoanalysis and the archaic conception of the bliss and perfection of the origin is based on the fact that Freud discovered the decisive role of the "primordial and paradisal time" of earliest childhood, the bliss before the break (= weaning), that is, before time becomes, for each individual, a "living time."

As for the second Freudian idea relevant to our investigation—that is, the "going back" by which one hopes to reconstitute certain decisive events of earliest childhod—it too supports a comparison with archaic behavior. We have cited a number of examples for the belief that one can reconstitute, and hence relive, the primordial events narrated in the myths. But with a few exceptions (among others, magical cures) these examples illustrate a *collective* "going back." It was the entire community, or a large part of the community, that rituals caused to relive the events reported in the myths. Psychoanalytic technique makes possible an *individual* return to the Time of the origin. Now, this existential going back is also known to archaic societies and plays an important part in certain psycho-physiological techniques of the East. It is to this problem that we shall now turn.

Traditional techniques for "going back"

We have no intention of comparing psychoanalysis with "primitive" or Eastern beliefs and techniques. The point of the comparison we shall make is to show that "going back," of which Freud saw the importance in understanding man and, especially, in healing him, was already practiced in non-European cultures. After all that we have said concerning the hope of renewing the World by repeating the cosmogony, it is not difficult to grasp the basis for these practices: the individual's return to the origin is conceived as an opportunity for renewing and regenerating the existence of him who undertakes it. But as we shall soon see, the "return to the origin" can be effected for a wide variety of purposes and can have many different meanings.

First and foremost, there is the well-known symbolism of initiation rituals implying a *regressus ad uterum*. Since we have studied this complex at length in our *Birth and Rebirth,* we will limit ourselves here to some brief indications. From the archaic stages of culture the initiation of adolescents includes a series of rites whose symbolism is crystal clear: through them, the novice is first transformed into an embryo and then is reborn. Initiation is equivalent to a second birth. It is through the agency of initiation that the adolescent becomes both a socially responsible and culturally awakened

being. The return to the womb is signified either by the
neophyte's seclusion in a hut, or by his being symbolically
swallowed by a monster, or by his entering a sacred spot
identified with the uterus of Mother Earth.[3]

What concerns us here is that, together with these puberty
rites typical of "primitive" societies, initiation rituals involving
a *regressus ad uterum* also exist in more complex cultures.
To confine ourselves, for the present, to India, the motif is
discernible in three different types of initiation ceremonies.
First there is the *upanayama* ceremony, that is, the boy's
introduction to his teacher. The motif of gestation and rebirth is clearly expressed in it: the teacher is said to transform
the boy into an embryo and to keep him in his belly for
three nights.[4] Whoever has gone through an *upanayama* is
"twice born" (*dvi-ja*). Next there is the *diksa* ceremony,
obligatory for one preparing to offer the *soma* sacrifice and
which, strictly speaking, consists in return to the foetal stage.[5]
Finally, the *regressus ad uterum* is similarly central to the
hiranya-garbha ceremony (literally, "golden foetus"). The
person undergoing the ceremony is put in a golden vessel in
the shape of a cow, and on emerging from it he is regarded
as a newborn infant.[6]

In all these cases the *regressus ad uterum* is accomplished
in order that the beneficiary shall be born into a new mode
of being or be regenerated. From the structural point of view,
the return to the womb corresponds to the reversion of the
Universe to the "chaotic" or embryonic state. The prenatal

[3] Cf., for example, the Australian Kunapipi ritual described, after R.
M. Berndt, in *Birth and Rebirth*, pp. 49 ff.
[4] Cf. *Birth and Rebirth*, pp. 53 ff.
[5] *Ibid.*, pp. 54 ff.
[6] *Ibid.*, pp. 56 ff.

darkness corresponds to the Night before Creation and to the darkness of the initiation hut.

Whether "primitive" or Indian, all these initiation rituals involving a return to the womb have, of course, a mythical model.[7] But even more interesting than the myths relating to initiation rites of *regressus ad uterum* are those that narrate the adventures of Heroes or of shamans and magicians who accomplished the *regressus* in their flesh-and-blood bodies, not symbolically. A large number of myths feature (1) a hero being swallowed by a sea monster and emerging victorious after breaking through the monster's belly; (2) initiatory passage through a *vagina dentata,* or the dangerous descent into a cave or crevice assimilated to the mouth or the uterus of Mother Earth. All these adventures are in fact initiatory ordeals, after accomplishing which the victorious hero acquires a new mode of being.[8]

The initiation myths and rites of *regressus ad uterum* reveal the following fact: the "return to the origin" prepares a new birth, but the new birth is not a repetition of the first, physical birth. There is properly speaking a mystical rebirth, spiritual in nature—in other words, access to a new mode of existence (involving sexual maturity, participation in the sacred and in culture; in short, becoming "open" to Spirit). The basic idea is that, to attain to a higher mode of existence, gestation and birth must be repeated; but they are repeated ritually, symbolically. In other words, we here have acts oriented toward the values of Spirit, not behavior from the realm of psycho-physiological activity.

---

[7] On the mythical model for Indian initiation rituals, cf. *Birth and Rebirth,* p. 55.

[8] *Ibid.,* pp. 64 ff.

We have found it necessary to dwell on this point to avoid leaving the impression that all myths and rites of "return to the origin" are on the same plane. To be sure, the symbolism is the same; but the contexts differ, and it is the intention shown by the context that gives us the true meaning in each case. As we saw, from the point of view of structure it is possible to homologize the prenatal darkness of the initiation hut with the Night before Creation. And, true enough, the Night from which the Sun is born every morning symbolizes the primordial Chaos, and the rising of the sun is a counterpart to the cosmogony. But obviously this cosmogonic symbolism is enriched with new values in the case of the birth of the mythical Ancestor, the birth of each individual, and initiatory rebirth.

All this will appear more clearly from the examples now to be discussed. We shall see that "return to the origin" has served as the model for physiological and psycho-mental techniques whose aim may be regeneration and longevity as it may be healing and final liberation. We have already had occasion to observe that the cosmogonic myth lends itself to various applications, among them healing, poetic creation, introducing the child into the society and culture, and so on. We have also seen that the *regressus ad uterum* can be homologized with a regression to the state of Chaos before the Creation. This being so, we understand why certain archaic therapies employ the ritual return to the womb instead of ceremonial recitation of the cosmogonic myth. In India, for example, even in our day traditional medicine effects rejuvenation of the aged and regeneration of dying patients by burying them in a grave shaped like a womb. The symbolism of "new birth" is obvious. The custom, moreover, is also documented outside of India: the sick are buried so that they may be born from the womb of Mother Earth.[9]

The "return to the origin" is also highly esteemed as therapy in China. Taoism lays considerable stress on "embryonic breathing," *t'ai-si*. It consists in a closed-circuit respiration like that of a foetus; the adept tries to imitate the circulation of blood and breath between mother and child and vice versa. The preface to the *T'ai-si k'eou kiue* ("Oral formulas for embryonic breathing") expressly states: "By going back to the base, by returning to the origin, one drives away old age, one returns to the state of a foetus."[10] A text from modern syncretistic Taoism runs: "That is why the (Buddha) Ju-lai (= Tathāgata), in his great mercy, revealed the method for the (alchemical) work by Fire and taught man to *re-enter the womb* in order to reconstitute his (true) nature and (the fullness of) his portion of life."[11]

Here, then, we have two different but related mystical techniques, both seeking to obtain the "return to the origin": "embryonic breathing" and the alchemical process. These two techniques are, of course, among the numerous methods employed by the Taoist to acquire youth and extreme longevity ("immortality"). Alchemical experimentation must be accompanied by an appropriate mystical meditation. During the fusion of metals the Taoist alchemist tries to bring about in his own body the union of the two cosmological principles, Heaven and Earth, in order to reproduce the primordial chaotic situa-

[9] *Patterns in Comparative Religion,* pp. 250 ff.

[10] H. Maspéro, "Les procédés de 'Nourrir le Principe Vital' dans la religion taoïste ancienne," *Journal Asiatique,* April-June, 1937, p. 198.

[11] *Houei-ming-king* by Lieou Houayang, cited by Rolf Stein, "Jardins en miniature d'Extrême Orient," *Bulletin de l'Ecole Française d'Extrême Orient* (Hanoi, 1943), vol. XLII, p. 97.

tion that existed before the Creation. This primordial situation (which, moreover, is called precisely the "chaotic" [*houen*] situation) corresponds both to the egg or the embryo and to the paradisal and innocent state of the uncreated World.[12] The Taoist endeavors to obtain this primordial state either by the meditation that accompanies alchemical experiment or by "embryonic breathing." But in the last analysis "embryonic breathing" amounts to what the texts call "unification of the breaths," a quite complex technique, which we cannot examine here. Suffice it to say that "unification of the breaths" has a cosmological model. For according to Taoist traditions, in the beginning the "breaths" were mingled and formed an egg, the Great-One, from which came Heaven and Earth.[13]

The ideal of the Taoists—that is, obtaining the bliss of youth and longevity ("immortality")—had, then, a cosmological model: the state of primordial unity. Here we no longer have a re-enactment of the cosmological myth, as in the healing rituals cited earlier. The aim is no longer to reiterate the *cosmic creation;* it is to recover the state that *preceded the cosmogony,* the state of "chaos." But the line of thought is the same: health and youth are obtained by a "return to the origin," be it "return to the womb" or return to the cosmic Great-One. So we may note the important fact that, in China too, sickness and old age are believed to be cured by "return to the origin," the only method that archaic thought considered able to annul the work of Time. For, in the end, it is always a matter of abolishing past Time, of "going back" and beginning life over again with all its virtualities intact.

[12] Cf. R. Stein, *op. cit.,* p. 54.
[13] H. Maspéro, *op. cit.,* p. 207, n. 1.

Curing oneself of the work of Time

India is especially interesting in this respect. There Yoga and Buddhism, developing certain psycho-physiological methods of "going back," elaborated them to a degree unknown elsewhere. Obviously the ritual no longer has a therapeutic purpose. *Regressus ad uterum* is no longer practiced to obtain a cure or a rejuvenescence or even symbolic repetition of the cosmogony intended to heal the patient by reimmersing him in the primordial fullness. Yoga and Buddhism are on a different plane from that of the primitive therapies. Their final goal is not health or rejuvenation but spiritual mastery and liberation. Yoga and Buddhism are soteriologies, mystical techniques, philosophies—and, naturally, pursue ends other than magical cures.

Nevertheless, it is impossible not to see that these Indian mystical techniques show structural analogies with the archaic therapies. The philosophies, the ascetic and contemplative techniques of India all pursue the same end—curing man of the pain of existence in Time.[14] For Indian thought, suffering is originated and indefinitely prolonged in the world by *karma*, by temporality; it is the law of *karma* that imposes the countless series of transmigrations, the eternal return to existence and hence to suffering. Liberation from the karmic law is equivalent to "cure." The Buddha is the "king of physicians," his message is proclaimed as a "new medicine." It is by "burning up" the very last germ of a future life that the individual definitively ends the karmic cycle and is delivered from Time. Now, one of the ways of "burning up" the karmic residues

[14] Cf. *Myths, Dreams and Mysteries,* pp. 49 ff.

is the technique of "going back" in order to learn one's previous lives. It is a pan-Indian technique. It is documented in the *Yoga-sūtras* (III, 18), it is known to all sages and contemplatives of the Buddha's period, and it is practiced and recommended by the Buddha himself.

"The method is to cast off from a precise instant of Time, the nearest to the present moment, and to retrace the Time backward (*pratiloman* or 'against the stream') in order to arrive *ad originem,* the point where existence first 'burst' into the world and unleashed Time. Then one rejoins that paradoxical instant before which Time was not, because nothing had been manifested. We can grasp the meaning and the aim of this technique: to re-ascend the stream of Time would necessarily bring one back ultimately to the point of departure, which coincides with that of the cosmogony. To re-live one's past lives would also be to understand them and, to a certain degree, 'burn up' one's 'sins'; that is, the sum of the deeds done in the state of ignorance and capitalized from one life to the next by the law of *karma*. But there is something of even greater importance: one attains to the beginning of Time and enters the Timeless—the eternal present which preceded the temporal experience inaugurated by the 'fall' into human existence. In other words, it is possible, starting from any moment of temporal duration, to exhaust that duration by retracing its course to the source and so come out into the Timeless, into eternity. But that is to transcend the human condition and regain the non-conditioned state, which preceded the fall into Time and the wheel of existences."[15]

Hatha-yoga and certain Tantric schools employ the method called "going against the current" (*ujāna sādhana*) or the

[15] *Ibid,* p. 50.

"regressive" (*ulta*) technique, in order to obtain the "inversion" of all the psycho-physiological processes. In the man who accomplishes it this "return" or "regression" finds expression in the annihilation of the Cosmos and hence brings about "emergence from Time," entrance into "immortality." Now, in the Tantric view immortality can be obtained only by *halting manifestation* and hence the process of disintegration; one must proceed "against the current" (*ujāna sādhana*) and recover the primordial Unity that existed *in illo tempore,* before the Creation.[16] What is necessary, then, is to enact in one's own being the process of cosmic resorption, and so return to the "origin." The *Shivasamhitā* (I, 69 f.) sets forth a significant spiritual exercise. After describing the creation of the Universe by Shiva, the text describes the inverse process of cosmic resorption, as it is to be *lived, experienced* by the yogi. The latter *sees* the element Earth become "subtle" and dissolve in the element Water, Water dissolve in Fire, Fire in Air, Air in Ether, and so on, until all is reabsorbed into the Great Brahman.[17] The yogi witnesses the *inverse of the process of Creation,* he "goes back" until he reaches the "origin." This yogic exercise may be compared with the Taoist technique for "returning to the egg" and the primordial Great-One.

To repeat: we have no intention of putting Indo-Chinese mystical techniques and primitive therapies on the same plane. They are different cultural phenomena. But it is interesting to observe a certain continuity of human behavior in respect to Time, both down the ages and in various cultures. This

---

[16] M. Eliade, *Yoga, Immortality and Freedom* (New York, 1958), pp. 270 ff.

[17] *Ibid.,* p. 272.

behavior may be defined as follows: *To cure the work of Time it is necessary to "go back" and find the "beginning of the World."* We have just seen that this "return to the origin" has been variously evaluated. In the archaic and paleo-Oriental cultures the reiteration of the cosmic myth had as its purpose abolishing past Time and beginning a new life with all vital forces intact. For the Chinese and Hindu "mystics" the goal ceased to be beginning a new life again here below, on earth, and became "going back" and reconstituting the primordial Great-One. But in these examples, as in all the others we have given, the characteristic and decisive element was always "returning to the origin."

Recovering the past

We have cited these few examples in order to compare two categories of techniques: (1) psychoanalysis and (2) archaic and Oriental methods involving different methods of "returning to the origin" (for a variety of ends). Our purpose was not to discuss these procedures at length, but to show that existential return to the origin, although typical of the archaic mentality, is not a form of behavior confined solely to that mentality. Freud elaborated an analogous technique to enable a modern individual to recover the content of certain "original" experiences. We have seen that there are several ways of "going back," but the most important are: (1) rapid and direct re-establishment of the first situation (whether Chaos or the precosmogonic state or the moment of Creation) and (2) progressive return to the "origin" by proceeding backward through Time from the present moment to the "absolute beginning." In the first case there is a vertiginously swift or even instantaneous abolition of the Cosmos (or of the human being as the result of a certain temporal duration) and restoration of the original situation ("Chaos" or—on the anthropological plane—the "seed," the "embryo"). There is an obvious resemblance between the structure of this method and that of the mythico-ritual scenarios of immediate regression to "Chaos" and reiteration of the cosmogony.

In the second case—that of gradual return to the origin—we have a meticulous and exhaustive recollecting of personal and historical events. To be sure, in these cases too the final goal is to "burn up" these memories, to abolish them as it were by reliving them and freeing oneself from them. But there is no longer an effort to blot them out instantaneously in order to return to the original moment as quickly as possible. On the contrary, the important thing is to recollect even the most insignificant details of one's life (present or past), for it is only by virtue of this recollection that one can "burn up" one's past, master it, keep it from affecting the present.

The difference from the first method, whose model is instantaneously abolishing the World and re-creating it, is obvious. Here *memory* plays the leading role. One frees oneself from the work of Time by recollection, by *anamnesis*. The essential thing is to remember all the events one has witnessed in Time. This technique, then, is related to the archaic conception that we discussed at length—the importance of knowing the origin and history of a thing in order to obtain mastery over it. To be sure, moving backward through Time implies an experience dependent on personal memory, whereas knowing the origin comes down to understanding a primordial exemplary history, a myth. But the structures are homologizable; it is always a matter of remembering, in clear and precise detail, *what happened in the beginning* and from then on.

Here we touch upon a problem of primary importance not only for the understanding of myth but especially for the later development of mythical thinking. Knowledge of the origin and exemplary history of things confers a sort of magical mastery over them. But this knowledge at the same time opens the way to systematic speculations on the origin and structures of the World. We shall return to this problem. But at this point we must note that memory is regarded as the pre-eminent form of knowledge. He who can *recollect* possesses an even more precious magico-religious power than he who *knows* the origin of things. In ancient India, for example, a clear distinction is made between "objective" knowledge of the origin of the various realities and "subjective" knowledge based on remembering earlier lives. "We know thy birthplace (*janitram*), O Dream," exclaims the author of a myth in the Atharva Veda (VI, 46, 2). "We know, O Agni, that thy birthplace is threefold" (*ibid.*, XIII, 3, 21). By virtue of this knowledge of the origin ("birthplace"), man can defend himself against dreams and can handle fire without being hurt.

But knowledge of one's own former lives—that is, of one's personal history—bestows even more: a soteriological knowledge and mastery over one's own destiny. He who remembers his "births" (origin) and his former lives (= periods made up of a considerable series of events undergone) succeeds in freeing himself from karmic conditionings; in other words, he becomes the master of his destiny. This is why "absolute memory"—such as the Buddha's, for example—is equivalent to omniscience and gives its possessor the powers of Cosmo-crator. Ananda and other disciples of the Buddha "remembered births," were among "those who remembered births." Vāma-deva, author of a famous Rig-Vedic hymn, said of himself: "Being in the womb, I knew all the births of the gods" (Rig Veda, IV, 27, 1). Krishna likewise "knows all existences" (Bhagavad-Gītā, IV, 5).[18] All alike—Gods, Buddhas, sages, yogis—are among *those who know*.

The knowledge of former lives is not an exclusively Indian technique. It is documented among shamans. We shall see that it plays an important part in Greek philosophical speculation. But what must be stressed now is the fact that the exceptional prestige accorded to knowledge of the "origins" and of ancient "history" (that is, of former lives) derives, in the last analysis, from the importance accorded to "existential" and "historical" myths, to myths narrating the constitution of the human condition. As we said, this condition has a "history"; certain decisive events took place during the mythical period, and it was after them that man became what he is at present. Now, this primordial dramatic and sometimes even tragic history must not only be *known,* it must be continually *recollected.* We shall later see the consequences of archaic man's thus deciding, at a certain moment in his history, that he would continually relive the crises and tragedies of his mythical past.

[18] Cf. *Myths, Dreams and Mysteries,* p. 51.

VI.

Mythology, Ontology, History

The essential precedes existence

FOR *homo religiosus* the essential precedes existence. This is as true of the man of "primitive" and Oriental societies as it is of the Jew, the Christian, and the Moslem. Man is what he is today because a series of events took place *ab origine*. The myths tell him these events and, in so doing, explain to him how and why he was constituted in this particular way. For *homo religiosus* real, authentic existence begins at the moment when this primordial history is communicated to him and he accepts its consequences. It is always sacred history, for the actors in it are Supernatural Beings and mythical Ancestors. For example: man is mortal because a mythical Ancestor stupidly lost immortality, or because a Supernatural Being decided to deprive him of it, or because a certain mythical event left him endowed at once with sexuality and mortality, and so on. Some myths explain the origin of death by an accident or an oversight: God's messenger, some animal, forgets the message, or lingers idly on the way, arrives too late, and so on. This is a plastic way of expressing the absurdity of death. But in this case too the story is still "Sacred History," because the author of the message is a Supernatural Being and, after all, if he had wanted to he could have annulled his messenger's mistake.

If it is true that the essential events took place *ab origine,* these events are not the same for all religions. For Judaeo-Christianity the "essential" is the drama of Paradise, which instituted the present human condition. For the Mesopotamian the "essential" is the formation of the World from the dismembered body of the sea monster Tiamat and the creation of man from the blood of the demon Kingu mixed with a little earth (in short, with a substance directly derived from the body of Tiamat). For an Australian the "essential" is nothing more than a series of acts performed by the Supernatural Beings in the "Dream Time."

There is not space here to enumerate all the mythical themes that, for the various religions, represent the "essential," the primordial drama that constituted man as he is today. It will be enough to mention the chief types. Then too, at this point in our investigation our first interest is to discover the attitudes that *homo religiosus* takes or has taken toward the "essential" that preceded him. We suppose *a priori* that there could have been several attitudes because, as we have just seen, the content of this "essential" which was determined in mythical Times varies from one religious vision to another.

Deus otiosus

Many primitive tribes, especially those arrested at the hunting and gathering stage, acknowledge the existence of a Supreme Being; but he plays almost no part in religious life. In addition, little is known about him, his myths are few and, in general, quite simple. This Supreme Being is believed to have created the World and man, but he soon abandoned his creations and withdrew into the Sky. Sometimes he did not even complete the Creation, and another Divine Being, his "Son" or his representative, took over the task. We have elsewhere discussed the transformation of the Supreme Being into a *deus otiosus;* here we shall confine ourselves to a few examples.[1] Among the Selk'nam of Tierra del Fuego the God, who is called "Inhabitant of the Sky" or "He who is in the Sky," is eternal, all-knowing, omnipotent, but the Creation was finished by the mythical Ancestors, whom the Supreme Being also created before he retired beyond the stars. This God lives apart from men, indifferent to what goes on in the World. He has no images and no priests. He is prayed to only in case of sickness ("O Thou on high, take not my child from me; he is still too little"), and offerings are made to him chiefly during storms.

The Yorubas of the Slave Coast believe in a Sky God named Olorum (literally, "Owner of the Sky") who, after beginning the Creation of the World, left it to a lesser god, Obatala, to finish and govern it. For his part, he withdrew once and for all from human and earthly affairs; and there are neither temples nor statues nor priests for this Supreme God who became a *deus otiosus*. He is nevertheless invoked as a last resort in times of calamity.

Withdrawn into the Sky, Ndyambi, the supreme god of the Hereros, has abandoned mankind to lesser divinities. "Why should we offer him sacrifices?" a native explains. "We have nothing to fear from him because, unlike our dead, he does us no harm."[2] The Supreme Being of the Tumbukas is too great "to be concerned with the ordinary affairs of men." Dzingbe ("the Universal Father") of the Ewe is invoked

[1] Cf. *Patterns in Comparative Religion,* pp. 46 ff.
[2] *Ibid.,* p. 48.

only during drought: "O sky, to whom we owe thanks, great is the drought; let it rain, let the earth be refreshed, let the fields prosper!"[3] The distance and indifference of the Supreme Being are admirably expressed in a saying of the East African Gyriamas, which depicts their god as follows: "Mulugu [God] is above, the ghosts are below!" The Bantus say: "God, after creating man, no longer cares for him." And the Pygmies repeat: "God has gone far from us!"[4]

As these few examples make clear, the Supreme Being seems to have lost *religious actuality;* he does not figure in cult and the myths show him as having withdrawn far from man- kind, he has become a *deus otiosus.* The phenomenon, be it said, is also found in the more complex religions of the ancient East and the Indo-Mediterranean world; the celestial Creator God, omniscient and all-powerful, is supplanted by a Fecun- dator God, consort of the Great Goddess, epiphany of the generative forces of the Universe.[5]

In some respects it could be said that the *deus otiosus* is the first example of the "death of God" that Nietzsche so frenziedly proclaimed. A Creator God who removes himself to a distance and disappears from cult is finally forgotten. Forgetfulness of God, like his own absolute transcendence, is a plastic expression of his religious nonactuality or, what amounts to the same thing, his "death." The disappearance of the Supreme Being did not find expression in an impover- ishment of religious life. On the contrary, it could be said that the genuine "religions" appear *after* he has vanished. The richest and most dramatic myths, the most extravagant

[3] *Ibid.,* p. 49.
[4] *Ibid.,* p. 49.
[5] Cf. *ibid.,* pp. 64 ff.

rituals, Gods and Goddesses of the most various kinds, the Ancestors, masks and secret societies, temples, priesthoods, and so on—all this is found in cultures that have passed beyond the stage of gathering and small-game hunting and in which the Supreme Being is either absent (forgotten?) or amalgamated with other Divine Figures to the point where he is no longer recognizable.

The "eclipse of God," in the terms of Martin Buber, the remoteness and silence of God that obsess certain contemporary theologians, are not modern phenomena. The "transcendence" of the Supreme Being has always served man as an excuse for indifference toward him. Even when man still remembers him, the fact that God is *so distant* justifies every kind of neglect if not complete unconcern. The Fang of Equatorial Africa put it simply but courageously:

> "God (Nzame) is above, man is below.
> God is God, man is man.
> Each in his own place, each in his house."[6]

The same view, as it happens, was held by Giordano Bruno: God "come absoluto, non ha che far con noi" (*Spaccio della bestia trionfante*).

One thing, however, should be noted: from time to time the forgotten or neglected Supreme Being is remembered, more especially in cases of a threat that comes from the celestial regions (drought, storm, epidemics, etc.). The reader may refer to the examples given above (pp. 94). In general, this forgotten God is only called upon as a last resort, when all approaches to other Divine Figures have failed. The Supreme God of the Oraons is Dharmesh. In moments of crisis

[6] *Ibid.,* p. 49.

a white cock is sacrificed to him, with the words: "Now we have tried every thing, but we still have you to help us! . . . God, thou art our Creator, have mercy on us!"[7] In the same way the Hebrews forsook Yahweh and took up with the Ba'als and Ashtartes whenever history made it possible, each time that they experienced a period of comparative peace and prosperity. But they were inevitably brought back to God by historical catastrophes. "And they cried unto the Lord, and said, We have sinned because we have forsaken the Lord, and have served Baalim and Ashtaroth: but now deliver us out of the hand of our enemies, and we will serve thee" (I Sam. 12:10).

But even when the Supreme God has completely disappeared from cult and is "forgotten," his memory survives, camouflaged and degraded, in the myths and tales of the primordial "Paradise," in the initiations and narratives of shamans and medicine men, in religious symbolism (symbols of the Center of the World, magical flight and ascension, sky and light symbols, etc.), and in certain types of cosmogonic myths. Much could be said on the problem of a Supreme Being being forgotten on the "conscious" level of collective religious life and of his larval survival on the level of the "unconscious" or on the plane of symbol or, finally, in the ecstatic experiences of some privileged individuals. But to discuss this problem would take us too far from our subject. We will only say that the survival of a Supreme Being in symbols or in individual ecstatic experiences is not without consequences for the religious history of archaic humanity. Sometimes such ecstatic experience or prolonged meditation on one of the celestial symbols will be enough to bring a strong religious personality

[7] J. G. Frazer, *The Worship of Nature* (London, 1926), p. 631.

to rediscover the Supreme Being. It is by virtue of such experiences and reflections that, in some cases, the entire community radically renews its religious life.

In general, for all these primitive cultures that have known a Supreme Being but have more or less forgotten him, the "essential" consists in these characteristic elements: (1) God created the World and man, then withdrew to the Sky; (2) his withdrawal was sometimes accompanied by a break in communications between Sky and Earth, or in a great increase in the distance between them; in some myths, the original nearness of the Sky and the presence of God on Earth constitute a paradisal syndrome (to which must be added man's original immortality, his friendly relations with the animals, and the absence of any need to work); (3) the place of this more or less forgotten *deus otiosus* was taken by various divinities, all of whom are closer to man and help him or persecute him in a more direct and constant way.

It is remarkable that the man of the archaic societies, who is generally so careful not to forget the acts of the Supernatural Beings as the myths record them for him, should have forgotten the Creator God transformed into a *deus otiosus*. The Creator survives in cult only when he appears in the form of a Demiurge or of a Supernatural Being who fashioned the tribe's familiar landscape (the "World"); this is the case in Australia. On the occasion of the ceremonies for renewing the World, this Supernatural Being is made ritually present. The reason is not far to seek: here the "Creator" is also the author of food. He not only created the World and the Ancestors, he also produced the animals and plants that enable man to live.[8]

[8] We should add, however, that Australia, too, has *dei otiosi;* cf. *Patterns . . .* , p. 43.

The murdered divinity

Besides the Supreme and Creator Gods who become *dei otiosi* and vanish, the history of religions knows Gods who disappear from the surface of the Earth, but disappear because they were put to death by men (more precisely, by the mythical Ancestors). Unlike the "death" of the *deus otiosus,* which leaves only a gap that is quickly filled by other religious Figures, the violent death of these divinities is *creative.* Something of great importance for human life appears as the result of their death. Nor is this all: the new thing thus shares in the substance of the slain divinity and hence in some sort continues his existence. Murdered *in illo tempore,* the divinity survives in the rites by which the murder is periodically re-enacted; or, in other cases, he survives primarily in the living forms (animals, plants) that sprang from his body.

The murdered divinity is *never* forgotten, though men may forget one or another detail of his myth. It is the less possible to forget him because it is primarily after his death that he becomes indispensable to mankind. We shall presently see that in many cases he is present in man's very body, especially through the foodstuffs that he eats. Furthermore, the death of the divinity radically changes man's mode of being. In some myths man, too, becomes mortal and sexed. In others the murder inspires the scenario of an initiatory ritual, that is, of the ceremony that transforms the "natural" man (the child) into cultural man.

The morphology of these divinities is extremely rich and their myths are numerous. Nevertheless, we find certain essential common features: these divinities *are not cosmogonic;* they appeared on Earth *after* the Creation and did not remain there long; murdered by men, they did not avenge themselves and did not even bear malice toward their murderers; on the contrary, they showed them how to profit by their death. The existence of these divinities is at once mysterious and dramatic. Usually their origin is not known; all that is known is that they came on Earth to be useful to men and that their great work derives directly from their violent death. It can be said, too, that these divinities are the first whose history anticipates human history; on the one hand, their existence is limited in Time; on the other, their tragic death goes to constitute the human condition.

In the present state of our knowledge it is difficult to determine at what stage of culture this type of divinity became clear-cut. As Jensen has shown, and as we shall presently see, the most characteristic examples occur among the palaeocultivators, that is, among the cultivators of tubers. But this type of divinity is also documented in Australia and, it seems, though very infrequently, among African hunters. An Australian myth runs as follows: An anthropomorphic giant, Lumaluma, who was at the same time a whale, came in from the shore and, traveling westward, devoured all the men he met on his way. The survivors wondered why they were becoming fewer. They began to watch, and found the whale on the shore with its belly full. The alarm being given, they gathered together and, the following morning, attacked the whale with lances. They opened its belly and took out the skeletons. The whale told them not to kill it, and before it died it would show them all the initiation rituals that it knew. The whale performed the *ma'raiin* ritual, showing men how they must dance and all the rest. "We do this," it said to them, "you do this; all this I give you, and I show you all this." After teaching them the *ma'raiin* ritual, the whale showed them others. Finally it went back into the sea and said: "Don't you call me Lumaluma any more. This time I change my name. You call me *nauwulnauwul* because I'm in the salt water now."[9]

The anthropomorphic giant-whale swallowed men to initiate them. Men did not know this, and killed it, but before "dying" (that is, before changing into a whale once and for all), Lumaluma revealed the initiation rituals to them. Now, these rituals more or less explicitly symbolize a death followed by a resurrection.

In the Australian Karadjeri tribe, the two Bagadjimbiri Brothers had a similar fate. In the "Dream Times" they came out of the ground in the form of dingos but then became two human giants. They altered the landscape and civilized the Karadjeri by showing them, among other things, the initiation rites. But a man (i.e., a mythical Ancestor) killed them with a lance. Resuscitated by their mother's milk, the Bagadjimbiri changed into water snakes, while their spirits went up to the Sky and became what Europeans call the Magellanic Clouds. Since then, the Karadjeri do exactly as the two mythical brothers did and meticulously imitate everything that they showed to the Ancestors, especially the initiation ceremonies.[10]

[9] R. M. Berndt and C. M. Berndt, *Sexual Behavior in Western Arnhem Land* (New York, 1955), pp. 139–141. Cf. also in *Birth and Rebirth,* p. 49, the myth of the python Lu'ningu which swallowed youths and vomited them up dead. Men killed it, but later commemorated it by a monument representing it—the two ritual posts that play a role in the secret Kunapipi ceremonial.

[10] R. Piddington, cited in *Myths, Dreams and Mysteries,* pp. 190 ff.

The African example now to be given is that of a secret society common to the Mandja and the Banda, but there is reason to believe that the same scenario is found on more archaic levels of culture. The society is named Ngakola and its initiation rituals re-enact the following myth: In times past Ngakola lived on Earth. His body was very black and covered with long hair. No one knew where he came from, but he lived in the bush. He had the power to kill a man and bring him back to life. He said to men: "Send me people, I will eat them and vomit them up renewed!" His advice was obeyed; but since Ngakola gave back only half of those he had swallowed, men decided to destroy him. They gave him "great quantities of manioc to eat in which stones had been mixed; thus they weakened the monster and were able to kill him with knives and assegais." This myth provides the basis for and justifies the rituals of the secret society. A flat sacred stone plays a great part in the ceremonies. According to tradition this sacred stone was taken from Ngakola's belly. The neophyte is put in a hut that symbolizes the monster's body. There he hears Ngakola's dismal voice, there he is whipped and tortured; for he is told that "he is now in Ngakola's belly" and being digested. The other initiates sing in chorus: "Ngakola, take our entrails, Ngakola, take our livers!" After other ordeals the master initiator finally announces that Ngakola, who had eaten the neophyte, has now vomited him up.[11]

As we said, this myth and ritual resemble other African initiations which are archaic in type. For African puberty rituals that include circumcision can be reduced to the follow-

[11] E. Anderson, cited in *Myths, Dreams and Mysteries*, pp. 204–205.

ing elements: The master initiators incarnate the divine Beasts of Prey and "kill" the novices by circumcising them; this initiatory murder is based on a myth that tells of a primordial Animal that killed men in order to bring them back to life "changed"; the Animal was itself finally killed, and this mythical event is ritually reiterated by the circumcision of the novices; "killed" by the wild beast of prey (represented by the master initiator), the novice later returns to life by putting on its skin.[12] ʹ

The mythico-ritual theme can be reconstructed as follows: "(1) A Supernatural Being kills men (to initiate them); (2) (not understanding the meaning of this initiatory death) men avenge themselves by slaying him; (3) but afterward they institute secret ceremonies related to this primordial drama; (4) the Supernatural Being is made present at these ceremonies through an image or sacred object supposed to represent his body or his voice."[13]

Hainuwele and the Dema

Myths of this class are characterized by the fact that the primordial murder of a Supernatural Being gave rise to initiation rituals by which men attain to a higher existence. It is also to be noted that the murder is not regarded as a crime; otherwise it would not have been periodically re-enacted in the rituals. This appears still more clearly from a study of the mythico-ritual complex typical of the palaeo-cultivators. A. E. Jensen has shown that the religious life among cultivators

[12] Cf. *Birth and Rebirth,* p. 24.
[13] *Ibid.,* p. 149, n. 28.

of tubers in tropical regions centers around divinities that he calls divinities of the *dema* type, the term *"dema"* being borrowed from the Marindanim of New Guinea. The Marindanim apply the term to the divine creators and Primordial Beings who existed in mythical Times. The *dema* are described sometimes in human form, sometimes in the form of animals and plants. The central myth narrates the slaying of the *dema*-divinity by the *dema*-men of the primordial Time.[14] Especially famous is the myth of the girl Hainuwele, recorded by Jensen in Ceram, one of the islands of the New Guinea Archipelago. In substance it runs:

In mythical Times a man named Ameta, out hunting, came on a wild boar. Trying to escape, the boar was drowned in a lake. On its tusk Ameta found a coconut. That night he dreamed of the coconut and was commanded to plant it, which he did the next morning. In three days a coconut palm sprang up, and three days later it flowered. Ameta climbed it to cut some flowers and make a drink from them. But he cut his finger and the blood dropped on a flower. Nine days later he found a girl-child on the flower. Ameta took her and wrapped her in coconut fronds. In three days the child became a marriageable girl, and he named her Hainuwele ("coconut branch"). During the great Maro festival Hainuwele stood in the middle of the dancing place and for nine nights distributed gifts to the dancers. But on the ninth day the men dug a grave in the middle of the dancing place and threw Hainuwele into it during the dance. The grave was filled in and men danced on it.

[14] A. E. Jensen, *Mythes et cultes chez les peuples primitifs,* trans. by M. Metzger and J. Goffinet (Paris, 1954), p. 108.

The next morning, seeing that Hainuwele did not come home, Ameta divined that she had been murdered. He found the body, disinterred it, and cut it into pieces, which he buried in various places, except the arms. The buried pieces gave birth to plants previously unknown, especially to tubers, which since then are the chief food of human beings. Ameta took Hainuwele's arms to another *dema*-divinity, Satene. Satene drew a spiral with nine turns on a dancing ground and placed herself at the center of it. From Hainuwele's arms she made a door, and summoned the dancers. "Since you have killed," she said, "I will no longer live here. I shall leave this very day. Now you will have to come to me through this door." Those who were able to pass through it remained human beings. The others were changed into animals (pigs, birds, fish) or spirits. Satene announced that after her going men would meet her only after their death, and she vanished from the surface of the Earth.[15]

A. E. Jensen has shown the importance of this myth for an understanding of the religion and World image of the palaeo-cultivators. The murder of a *dema* divinity by the *dema,* the Ancestors of present humanity, ends an epoch (which cannot be considered "paradisal") and opens that in which we live today. The *dema* became men, that is, sexed and mortal

[15] A. E. Jensen, *Das religiöse Weltbild einer frühen Kultur* (Stuttgart, 1948), pp. 35–38; cf. also Joseph Campbell, *The Masks of God: Primitive Mythology* (New York, 1959), pp. 173–176. On the dissemination of this mythical motif, cf. Gudmund Hatt, "The Corn Mother in America and Indonesia," *Anthropos,* vol. XLVI (1951), pp. 853–914. Hermann Baumann's objections (cf. *Das doppelte Geschlecht* [Berlin 1955]) have been discussed by A. E. Jensen in his article "Der Anfang des Bodenbaus in mythologischer Sicht," *Paideuma,* vol. VI (1956), pp. 169–180. See also Carl A. Schmitz, "Die Problematik der Mythologeme 'Hainuwele' and 'Prometheus,'" *Anthropos,* vol. LV (1960), pp. 215–238.

beings. As for the murdered *dema*-divinity, she survives both
in her own "creations" (food, plants, animals, etc.) and in
the house of the dead into which she was changed, or in the
"mode of being of death," which she established by her own
demise. We could say that the *dema*-divinity "camouflages"
her existence in the various modes of existing that she inaugurated by her violent death: the underground realm of the
dead, the plants and animals that sprang from her dismembered body, sexuality, the new kind of existence on Earth
(that is, being mortal). The violent death of the *dema*-
divinity is not only a "creative" death, it is also a way of
being continually present in the life of men and even in their
death. For by feeding on the plants and animals that sprang
from her body, men actually feed on the very substance of
the *dema*-divinity. Hainuwele, for example, survives in the
coconut, the tubers, and the pigs that men eat. But, as Jensen
has well shown,[16] slaughtering the pig is a "re-presentation"
of Hainuwele's murder. And its repetition has no other meaning than to recall the divine exemplary act that gave birth
to everything that exists on Earth today.

For the paleo-cultivators, then, the "essential" is concen-
trated in this primordial murder. And since religious life
consists primarily in recalling this act, the worst sin is to
"forget" any episode of the primordial divine drama. The
different moments of religious life continually evoke the event
that took place *in illo tempore* and thus help man to remain
conscious of the divine origin of the present World. As Jensen
says,[17] the *puberty ceremonies* recall the fact that man's
capacity to procreate derives from the first mythical murder,

16 Cf. *Mythes et cultes chez les peuples primitifs*, pp. 189 ff.
17 *Ibid.*

and at the same time show that mortality is inseparable from procreation. The *funeral ceremonies,* which are concerned with the journey of the deceased to the realm of the dead, recall that the journey is only a repetition of the first such journey, performed by the *dema*-divinity. But it is the reiteration of the slaying of the *dema*-divinity that constitutes the essential element. *Human sacrifices* or *animal sacrifices* are only a solemn commemoration of the primordial murder. And *cannibalism* is explained by the same idea that is implicit in the eating of tubers—that, in one way or another, men are always eating the divinity.

The religious ceremonies are, then, festivals of memory. "Knowing" means learning the central myth (the murder of the divinity and its consequences) and endeavoring never to forget it. The real sacrilege is to *forget* the divine act. "Wrong," "sin," "sacrilege" is "not remembering" that the present form of human existence is the result of a divine act. For example, among the Wemale the Moon is a *dema*-divinity; it is believed to have its menstrual period at the new moon and to remain invisible for three nights. This is why menstruating women are isolated in special huts. Any infraction of this interdict requires an expiatory ceremony. The woman brings an animal to the cult house, where the influential men are gathered, confesses her guilt, and goes away. The men sacrifice the animal, roast it, and eat it. This killing rite is a commemoration of the first blood sacrifice, that is, of the primordial murder. "The sacrilege of *not having remembered* is logically expiated by *remembering with special intensity.* And because of its original meaning, blood sacrifice is a particularly intense 'reminder' of this sort."[18]

[18] *Ibid.,* p. 225.

"Ontology" gives place to "History"

From the structural point of view, all these myths are origin myths. They reveal the origin of man's present condition, of food plants and animals, of death, of religious institutions (puberty initiations, secret societies, blood sacrifices, etc.) and of rules of human conduct and behavior. For all these religions the "essential" was not fixed at the Creation of the World but after it, at a certain moment of the mythical period. A mythical Time is still involved, but it is no longer the "first" Time, what we may call the "cosmogonic" Time. The "essential" is no longer bound up with an *ontology* (how the World—the real—came into being) but with a *History*. It is a History at once divine and human, for it is the result of a drama acted out by the Ancestors of men and by Supernatural Beings different in type from the all-powerful, immortal Creator Gods. These Divine Beings are subject to changes in modality; they "die" and become something else, but this "death" is not an annihilation, they do not perish once and for all, but survive in their creations. Nor is this all. For their death at the hands of the mythical Ancestors changed not only *their* mode of being but the mode of being of *mankind*. From the time of the primordial murder an indissoluble relation arose between Divine Beings of the *dema* type and men. Between them at present there is a sort of "communion": man feeds on the God and, when he dies, joins him again in the realm of the dead.

These are the first pathetic and tragic myths. In later cultures—the so-called "culture of the Masters" and, later, the urban cultures of the ancient Near East—other pathetic and violent mythologies will develop. It is not within the scheme of this short book to examine them all. We may say here, however, that the celestial Supreme Being and Creator recovers his religious activity only in certain pastoral cultures (especially among the Turco-Mongols) and in the monotheism of Moses, in the reform of Zarathustra, and in Islam. Even when his name is still remembered—Anu of the Mesopotamians, El of the Canaanites, Dyaus of the Vedic Indians, Ouranos of the Greeks—the Supreme Being no longer plays an important role in religious life and is but little represented in mythology (sometimes he is completely absent from it—e.g., Dyaus). The "passivity" of Ouranos as *deus otiosus* is plastically expressed by his castration: he has become "impotent" and unable to take part in the affairs of the World. In Vedic India Varuna supplanted Dyaus, but he in his turn first gives way before a young warrior god, Indra, then is completely supplanted by Vishnu and Shiva. El yields the primacy to Ba'al as Anu does to Marduk. Except for Marduk, all these Supreme Gods are no longer "creative" in the active sense. They did not create the World, they only organized it and assumed the responsibility for maintaining order and fertility in it. Primarily, they are Fecundators, like Zeus or Ba'al who, by their hierogamies with the Earth goddesses, ensure the fertility of the fields and the abundance of harvests.[19] Marduk himself is not the creator of *this World,* of the Universe as it exists today. Another "World"—almost unthinkable for us, because fluid, an Ocean not a Cosmos—existed before this one: it was the World ruled by Tiamat and her Spouse, in which three generations of God lived.

These few indications will suffice. What must be stressed is the fact that the great mythologies of Euro-Asiatic poly-

[19] Cf. *Patterns in Comparative Religion,* pp. 64–93.

theism, which correspond to the first historical civilizations, are increasingly concerned with what happened *after* the Creation of the Earth, and even after the creation (or the appearance) of man. The accent is now on what *happened to* the Gods and no longer on what they *created*. To be sure, there is always a more or less clearly "creative" aspect in every divine adventure—but what appears more and more important is no longer the *result* of the adventure but the *sequence of dramatic events* that constitute it. The countless adventures of Ba'al, of Zeus, of Indra, or those of their colleagues in the respective pantheons, represent the most "popular" mythological themes.

Mention must also be made of the pathetic myths of the young Gods who die murdered or by accident (Osiris, Tammuz, Attis, Adonis, etc.) and sometimes come back to life, or of a Goddess who goes down to Hades (Ishtar), or of a divine Maiden who is forced to descend there (Persephone). These "deaths," like Hainuwele's, are "creative" in the sense that they bear some relation to vegetation. Around one of these violent deaths or the descent of a divinity to Hell the Mystery religions will later grow up. But these deaths, though pathetic, did not inspire rich and diversified mythologies. Like Hainuwele, these Gods who die and (sometimes) return to life exhausted their dramatic destiny in the one central episode. And, like Hainuwele's, their death is significant for the human condition: ceremonies related to vegetation (Osiris, Tammuz, Persephone, etc.) or initiatory institutions (Mysteries) arose as the result of this tragic event.

The great mythologies—those consecrated by such poets as Homer and Hesiod and the anonymous bards of the Mahābhārata, or elaborated by ritualists and theologians (as in Egypt, India, and Mesopotamia)—are more and more inclined to narrate the *gesta* of the Gods. And at a certain moment in History—especially in Greece and India but also in Egypt—an elite begins to lose interest in this *divine history* and arrives (as in Greece) at the point of no longer believing in the *myths* while claiming still to believe in the *Gods*.

The beginnings of "demythicization"

The history of religions here finds the first example of a conscious and definite process of "demythicization." To be sure, even in the archaic cultures a myth would sometimes be emptied of religious meaning and become a legend or a nursery tale; but other myths remained in force. In any case, there was no question here, as there was in Pre-Socratic Greece and Upanishadic India, of a cultural phenomenon of the first importance, whose consequences have proved to be incalculable. For after this "demythicization" process the Greek and Brahmanic mythologies could no longer represent for the respective elites of those countries what they had represented for their forefathers.

For these elites the "essential" was no longer to be sought in the history of the Gods but in a "primordial situation" preceding that history. We witness an attempt to go beyond mythology as divine history and to reach a primal source from which the real had flowed, to identify the womb of Being. It was in seeking the source, the principle, the *arche,* that philosophical speculation for a short time coincided with cosmogony; but it was no longer the cosmogonic myth, it was an ontological problem.

The "essential" is reached, then, by a prodigious "going

back"—no longer a *regressus* obtained by ritual means, but
a "going back" accomplished by an effort of thought. In this
sense it could be said that the earliest philosophical speculations derive from mythologies: systematic thought endeavors
to identify and understand the "absolute beginning" of which
the cosmogonies tell, to unveil the mystery of the Creation
of the World, in short, the mystery of the appearance of Being.

But we shall see that the "demythicization" of Greek religion and the triumph, with Socrates and Plato, of strict and
systematic philosophy, did not finally do away with mythical
thought. Then too, it is difficult to imagine a radical out-
moding of mythological thought as long as the prestige of the
"origins" remains intact and as long as *forgetting* what took
place *in illo tempore*—or in a transcendental World—is regarded as the chief obstacle to knowledge or salvation. We shall
see to what an extent Plato is still a partisan of this archaic
mode of thought. And venerable mythological themes still
survive in the cosmology of Aristotle.

In all probability, the Greek genius left to itself and its own
devices could not have exorcised mythical thought, even if
the last God had been dethroned and his myths brought
down to the level of children's tales. For, on the one hand,
the Greek philosophical genius accepted the essence of mythical
thought, the eternal return of things, the cyclic vision of
cosmic and human life, and, on the other hand, the Greek
mind did not consider that History could become an object
of knowledge. Greek physics and metaphysics developed some
basic themes of mythical thought: the importance of the
origin, the *arche;* the essential that precedes human existence;
the determinative role of memory, and so on. This, of course,
does not mean that there is no solution of continuity between

Greek myth and philosophy. But we can easily understand that philosophical thought could employ and continue the mythical vision of cosmic reality and human existence.

It is only through the discovery of History—more precisely by the awakening of the historical consciousness in Judaeo-Christianity and its propagation by Hegel and his successors —it is only through the radical assimilation of the new mode of being represented by human existence in the World that myth could be left behind. But we hesitate to say that mythical thought has been abolished. As we shall soon see, it managed to survive, through radically changed (if not perfectly camouflaged). And the astonishing fact is that, more than anywhere else, it survives in historiography!

VII.

Mythologies of Memory and Forgetting

When a yogi falls in love with a queen . . .

MATSYENDRANĀTH and Gorakhnāth are among the most popular master yogis of the Indian Middle Ages. Their magical exploits have brought forth a rich and extensive epic literature. One of the central episodes of this mythological folklore is the amnesia of Matsyendranāth. According to one of the best-known versions the master, traveling in Ceylon, fell in love with the queen and went to live in her palace, completely forgetting his identity. A Nepalese variant relates that Matsyendranāth succumbed to temptation in the following way: while his body lay guarded by a disciple, his spirit entered the corpse of a king who had just died and restored it to life. (This is the well-known yogic miracle of "entering another's body"; the saints sometimes make use of this method to enjoy the pleasures of love without polluting themselves.) Finally, according to the poem *Goraksha-vijaya*, Matsyendranāth was made a prisoner by the women of the country of Kadalī.

On receiving news of his captivity, Gorakhnāth realizes that his master is doomed to die. He accordingly descends into the realm of Yama (Death), searches the Book of Fates, finds the leaf containing the destiny of his *guru,* and erases his name from the list of the dead. "He then goes to Matsyen-dranāth, in Kadalī, presenting himself under the form of a dancing girl, and falls to dancing, at the same time singing enigmatic songs. Little by little, Matsyendranāth remembers his true identity; he understands that the 'way of the flesh' leads to death, that his 'oblivion' was, basically, forgetfulness of his true and immortal nature, and that the 'charms of Kadalī' represent the mirages of profane life."[1] Gorakhnāth urges him to return to the way of Yoga and make his body "perfect." He tells him that it was Durgā who had brought on the "forgetfulness" that had almost cost him immortality. The spell, Gorakhnāth adds, symbolizes the eternal curse of ignorance laid on the human being by "Nature" (that is, Durgā).[2]

This mythical theme can be analyzed into the following elements: (1) A spiritual Master falls in love with a queen or is made prisoner by women; (2) in either case, there is a physical love that immediately provokes a state of amnesia in the Master; (3) his disciple seeks him out and, through a series of symbols (dance movements, secret signs, mysterious language), helps him to recover his memory, that is, con-sciousness of his identity; (4) the Master's "forgetfulness" is assimilated to death, and—vice versa—his "awakening," or *anamnesis,* proves to be a prerequisite for immortality.

The central motif—especially the amnesia-captivity brought on by an immersion in Life, and the *anamnesis* procured by the signs and mysterious words of a disciple—rather suggests the celebrated Gnostic myth of the "Saved Saviour," as found

[1] M. Eliade, *Yoga, Immortality and Freedom* (New York, 1958), p. 314.
[2] *Ibid.,* p. 314.

in the *Hymn of the Pearl*. As we shall see later, there are also other analogies between certain aspects of Indian thought and Gnosticism. But in this particular case there is no need to assume any Gnostic influence. Matsyendranāth's captivity and forgetting are a pan-Indian motif. Both misfortunes plastically express the fall of the spirit (the Self; *ātman, purusha*) into the circle of existences and, as a consequence, loss of consciousness of the Self. Indian literature uses images of binding, chaining, and captivity interchangeably with those of forgetting, unknowing, and sleep to signify the human condition; contrariwise, images of being freed from bonds and the tearing of a veil (or the removal of a bandage from the eyes), of memory, remembering, being awakened, the waking state, express abolishing (or transcending) the human condition, freedom, deliverance (*moksa, mukti, nirvāna,* etc.).

Indian symbolism of forgetting and recollection

The *Dīghanikāya* (I, 19–22) affirms that the Gods fall from Heaven when their "memory fails and they are of confused memory"; on the contrary, those Gods who do not forget are immutable, eternal, of a nature that knows no change. "Forgetting" is equivalent, on the one hand, to "sleep" and, on the other, to loss of the self, that is, to disorientation, blindness (having the eyes blindfolded). The *Chandogya Upanishad* (VI, 14, 1–2) tells of a man whom bandits carried far from his city, blindfolded, and abandoned in a lonely place. The man begins to cry: "I have been led here with my eyes bandaged, I have been left here with my eyes bandaged!" Someone removes the blindfold and points out the direction of his city. Asking his way from village to village, the man manages to reach home. In the same way, the text adds, he who has a competent Master becomes able to free himself from the blindfolds of ignorance and inevitably attains perfection.

Sankara's commentary on this passage is famous. It is the same, he explains, with the man carried by thieves far from Being (that is, from the *ātman-Brahman*) and trapped in this body. The thieves are the false ideas of "merit, demerit," and the like. His eyes are blindfolded with the blindfold of illusion, and he is hobbled by his desire for his wife, his son, his friends, his cattle, and so on. "I am the son of so-and-so, I am happy, or unhappy, I am intelligent, or stupid, I am pious, etc. How shall I live? where is there a way of escape? where is my salvation?" So he cries out, caught in a monstrous net—until the moment when he meets one who is conscious of true Being (*Brahman-ātman*), who is freed from slavery, happy, and, in addition, full of sympathy for others. From him he learns the way of knowledge and the vanity of the world. Thus the man who was the prisoner of his own illusions is liberated from dependence on worldly things. Then he recognizes his true Being and understands that he is not the lost wanderer he had thought himself to be. On the contrary, he understands that what Being is, is the very same thing that he, too, is. His eyes are freed from the bandage of illusion created by ignorance (*avidyā*), and he is like the man from Gandhāra returning home, that is, rediscovering the *ātman,* full of joy and serenity.[3]

We recognize the clichés through which Indian speculation attempts to make the paradoxical situation of the Self comprehensible: entangled in the illusions created and fed by its

---

[3] Sankara, commentary on the *Chandogya Upanishad,* VI, 14, 1–2.

temporal existence, the Self (*ātman*) suffers the consequences of this "ignorance" until the day it discovers that it was only *seemingly* involved in the World. Sāmkhya and Yoga take a similar position: the Self (*purusha*) is only apparently enslaved, and liberation (*mukti*) is simply its *becoming conscious* of its eternal freedom. "*I* believe that I suffer, *I* believe that I am bound, *I* desire liberation. At the moment when—having 'awakened'—I understand that this 'I' is a product of matter (*prakrti*), I at the same time understand that all existence has been only a chain of moments of suffering and that true Spirit 'impassively contemplated' the drama of 'personality.' "[4]

It is of importance to note that for Sāmkhya-Yoga, as well as for Vedānta, liberation can be compared to an "awakening" or to a new consciousness of a situation that existed from the beginning but that one was unable to *realize*. From a certain point of view "ignorance"—which, in the last analysis, is an *ignorance of oneself*—can be thought of as a "forgetting" of the true Self (*ātman, purusha*). "Wisdom" (*jñāna, vidyā,* etc.), which by tearing the veil of *māyā* or overcoming ignorance makes liberation possible, is an "awakening." The Awakened One par excellence, the Buddha, possesses absolute omniscience. We saw in an earlier chapter that, like other sages and yogis, Buddha remembered his former lives. But, the Buddhist texts insist, while the sages and yogis were able to remember a certain number of existences, even a considerable number, only the Buddha was able to know them *all*. This is a way of saying that only the Buddha was omniscient.

[4] M. Eliade, *op. cit.,* p. 31.

"Forgetfulness" and "Memory" in ancient Greece

Memory, Plotinus held, is for those who have forgotten (*Enneads* 4, 3, 25 ff.). The doctrine is Platonic: For those who have forgotten, remembering is a virtue; but the perfect never lose the vision of truth and they have no need to remember (*Phaedrus* 250). Hence there is a difference between memory (*mnemne*) and recollection (*anamnesis*). The Gods of whom the Buddha spoke in the *Dīghanikāya,* who fell from heaven when their memories were troubled, were reincarnated as men. Some of them practiced asceticism and meditation, and by virtue of their yogic discipline succeeded in recollecting their former lives. A perfect memory, then, is superior to the ability to recollect. In one way or another, recollecting implies having forgotten, and in India, as we just saw, forgetting is equivalent to ignorance, slavery (captivity), and death.

A like situation obtained in Greece. We have no intention of presenting all the data for "forgetfulness" and *anamnesis* in Greek beliefs and speculation. We shall only undertake to trace the various modifications of the "mythology of memory and forgetting," whose great role among protoagricultural societies we saw in the preceding chapter. In India, as in Greece, beliefs more or less similar to those of the protoagriculturalists were analyzed, reinterpreted, and revalued by poets, contemplatives, and the earliest philosophers. In India and Greece, that is, we no longer have to deal only with religious patterns of behavior and mythological expressions, but instead, and above all, with the rudiments of psychology and metaphysics. Nevertheless, there is continuity between the "popular" beliefs and the "philosophic" speculations. It is this continuity which is of particular concern to us.

The Goddess Mnemosyne, personification of "Memory," sister of Kronos and Okeanos, is the mother of the Muses. She is omniscient; according to Hesiod (*Theogony* 32, 38), she knows "all that has been, all that is, all that will be." When the poet is possessed by the Muses, he draws directly from Mnemosyne's store of knowledge, that is, especially from the knowledge of "origins," of "beginnings," of genealogies. "The Muses sing, beginning with the beginning—*ex arkhes* (*Theog*. 45, 115)—the first appearance of the world, the genesis of the gods, the birth of humanity. The past thus revealed is much more than the antecedent of the present; it is its source. In going back to it, recollection does not seek to situate events in a temporal frame but to reach the depths of being, to discover the original, the primordial reality from which the cosmos issued and which makes it possible to understand becoming as a whole."[5]

By virtue of the primordial memory that he is able to recover, the poet inspired by the Muses has access to the original realities. These realities were manifested in the mythical Times of the beginning and constitute the foundation of this World. But just because they appeared *ab origine*, they are no longer perceivable in current experience. J. P. Vernant rightly compares the poet's inspiration to an "evocation" of a dead person from the world below or to a *descensus ad inferos* undertaken by a living man in order to learn what he seeks to know. "The privilege that Mnemosyne confers on the

---

[5] J. P. Vernant, "Aspects mythiques de la mémoire en Grèce," *Journal de Psychologie* (1959), p. 7. Cf. also Ananda K. Coomaraswamy, "Recollection, Indian and Platonic," Supplement to the *Journal of the American Oriental Society*, No. 3 (April-June, 1944).

bard is that of a contact with the other world, the possibility of entering it and freely returning from it. The past appears as a dimension of the beyond."[6]

This is why, in so far as it is "forgotten," the "past"—historical or primordial—is homologized with death. The fountain Lethe, "forgetfulness," is a necessary part of the realm of Death. The dead are those who have lost their memories. On the other hand, certain privileged mortals, like Tiresias or Amphiaraus, preserve their memory after death. To make him immortal, Hermes gives his son Aethalides "an unchangeable memory." According to Apollonius of Rhodes, even when he crossed Acheron, forgetfulness did not submerge his soul; and though he inhabits now the realm of shades, now that of the sun's light, he always remembers what he has seen.[7]

But the "mythology of Memory and Forgetting" changes, and becomes enriched by an eschatological meaning, when a doctrine of transmigration takes shape. It is no longer the primordial past, but the series of *former personal lives* of which a knowledge is important. The function of Lethe is reversed. The soul newly freed from the body no longer finds in its waters forgetfulness of earthly life. On the contrary, Lethe blots out memory of the celestial world in the soul returning to earth to be reincarnated. "Forgetting" no longer symbolizes death, but returning to life. The soul that has been rash enough to drink from the fount of Lethe ("gorged with forgetfulness and vice," as Plato puts it, *Phaedrus* 248 c), is reincarnated and again cast into the cycle of becoming. In the gold plates worn by initiates in the Orphico-Pythag-

---

[6] J. P. Vernant, *op. cit.*, p. 8.
[7] *Argonautica*, I, 643, quoted by Vernant, *op. cit.*, p. 10.

orean brotherhood, the soul is commanded not to approach the spring of Lethe, on the left-hand road, but to take the road to the right, where it will find the spring that comes from the lake of Mnemosyne. "Quickly give me the fresh water that flows from the lake of Memory," the soul is told to ask the guardians of the spring. "And of themselves they will give you water from the sacred spring and, after that, among the other heroes you will be the master."[8]

Pythagoras, Empedocles, and others believed in metempsychosis and claimed that they could remember their former lives. "A wanderer exiled from the divine dwelling," Empedocles said of himself, "in former times I was already a boy and a girl, a bush and a bird, a mute fish in the sea" (*Purifications* fr. 117). And further: "I am delivered forever from death" (*ibid.*, fr. 112). Speaking of Pythagoras, Empedocles described him as "a man of extraordinary knowledge," for "wherever he directed all the power of his spirit, he easily saw what he had been there in ten, twenty human lives" (*ibid.*, fr. 129). Then too, memory-training played an important role in the Pythagorean brotherhoods (Diodorus X, 5; Iamblichus, *Vita Pyth.* 78 ff.). This training is reminiscent of the yogic technique of "going back" which we discussed in Chapter V. We may add that shamans, too, claim to remember their former lives,[9] which indicates the archaism of the practice.

[8] Plates from Petelia and Eleuthernae. On the "Orphic" plates, cf. Jane Harrison, *Prolegomena to the Study of Greek Religion* (Cambridge, 1903), pp. 573 ff.; F. Cumont, *Lux perpetua* (Paris, 1949), pp. 248, 406; W. K. C. Guthrie, *Orpheus and the Greek Religion* (London, 1935; 2nd ed., 1952), pp. 171 ff.

[9] Cf. M. Eliade, *Myths, Dreams and Mysteries*, pp. 162 ff. On the former lives of Pythagoras, cf. the texts assembled by E. Rohde, *Psyche*, trans. by W. B. Hillis (New York, 1925), pp. 598 ff.

"Primordial" memory and "historical" memory

In Greece, then, there are two evaluations of memory: (1) that which refers to primordial events (cosmogony, theogony, genealogy), and (2) the memory of former lives, that is, of historical and personal events. Lethe, "Forgetfulness," has equal efficacy against the two kinds of memory. But Lethe is powerless in the case of certain privileged persons: (1) those who, inspired by the Muses or by virtue of a "power of prophecy in reverse," succeed in recovering the memory of primordial events; (2) those who, like Pythagoras or Empedocles, are able to remember their former lives. These two categories of privileged persons overcome "forgetfulness," which is in some sort equivalent to overcoming death. The former class attain to the knowledge of "origins" (origin of the Cosmos, of the Gods, of peoples, of dynasties). The others remember their "history," that is, their transmigrations. For the former, the important thing is what took place *ab origine*. This consisted in primordial events, in which they were not personally involved. But these events—cosmogony, theogony, genealogy—in some sort constituted them; they are what they are because these events took place. It is unnecessary to show to what an extent this attitude resembles that of the man of archaic societies, who accepts himself as constituted by a series of primordial events set forth in the myths.

Those, on the other hand, who are able to remember their former lives are above all concerned with discovering their own "history," parceled out as it is among their countless incarnations. They try to unify these isolated fragments, to make them parts of a single pattern, in order to discover the direction and meaning of their destiny. For the unification, through *anamnesis,* of these totally unrelated fragments of history also implies "joining the beginning to the end"; in other words, it is necessary to discover how the first earthly existence set in motion the process of transmigration. Such a concern and such a discipline suggest the Indian techniques of "going back" and recollecting former lives.

Plato knows and employs these two traditions concerning memory and forgetfulness. But he transforms and reinterprets them to fit them into his philosophical system. For Plato, learning is, in the last analysis, recollecting (cf. especially *Meno* 81, c, d). Between two existences on earth the soul contemplates the Ideas: it shares in pure and perfect knowledge. But when the soul is reincarnated it drinks of the spring Lethe and forgets the knowledge it obtained from direct contemplation of the Ideas. Yet this knowledge is latent in the man in whom the soul is reincarnated, and it can be made patent by philosophical effort. Physical objects help the soul to withdraw into itself and, through a sort of "going back," to rediscover and repossess the original knowledge that it possessed in its extraterrestrial condition. Hence death is the return to a primordial and perfect state, which is periodically lost through the soul's reincarnation.

We have already had occasion to compare Plato's philosophy with what could be termed "archaic ontology."[10] We must now show in what sense Plato's theory of Ideas and the Platonic *anamnesis* can be compared with the attitude and behavior of man in archaic and traditional societies. The man of those societies finds in myths the exemplary models for all his acts. The myths tell him that everything he does or intends to do *has already been done,* at the beginning of Time,

[10] Cf. *The Myth of the Eternal Return,* pp. 34 ff.

in illo tempore. Hence myths constitute the sum of useful knowledge. An individual life becomes, and remains, a fully human, responsible, and significant life to the extent to which it is inspired by this stock of acts already performed and thoughts already formulated. Not to know or to forget the contents of the "collective memory" constituted by tradition is equivalent to a retrogression to the "natural" state (the acultural condition of the child), or to a "sin," or to a disaster.

For Plato, living intelligently, that is, learning to know and knowing the true, the beautiful, and the good, is above all remembering a disincarnate, purely spiritual existence. "Forgetting" this pleromatic condition is not necessarily a "sin" but is a consequence of the process of reincarnation. It is remarkable that, for Plato too, "forgetting" is not a necessary concomitant of the fact of death but, on the contrary, is related to life, to reincarnation. It is in returning to earthly life that the soul "forgets" the Ideas. Here we find not a forgetting of previous lives—that is, of the sum of personal experiences, of "history"—but a forgetting of transpersonal and eternal truths, the Ideas. Philosophical *anamnesis* does not recover the memory of the *events* belonging to former lives, but of *truths,* that is, the structures of the real. This philosophical position can be compared with that of the traditional societies: the myths represent paradigmatic models established by Supernatural Beings, not the series of personal experiences of one individual or another.[11]

[11] Cf. *Myths, Dreams and Mysteries,* pp. 54–55. For C. G. Jung too, the "collective unconscious" precedes the individual psyche. The world of Jung's archetypes to some extent resembles the world of the Platonic Ideas: the archetypes are transpersonal and do not take part in the historical Time of the individual but in the Time of the species, or even of organic life.

Sleep and Death

In Greek mythology, Sleep and Death, Hypnos and Thanatos, are twin brothers. We may note that, for the Jews too, at least from postexilic times on, death was comparable to sleep. Sleep in the grave (Job 3:13–15; 3:17), in Sheol (Eccles. 9:3; 9:10), or in both at once (Ps. 88 [87]). The Christians accepted and elaborated the homology of death and sleep: *in pace bene dormit, dormit in somno pacis, in pace somni, in pace Domini dormias* are among the most frequent formulas.[12]

Since Hypnos is brother to Thanatos, we see why, in Greece as in India and in Gnosticism, the act of "awakening" had a "soteriological" meaning (in the broadest sense of the word). Socrates awakens those who talk with him, even though against their will. "How tyrannical you are, Socrates!" Callicles exclaims (*Gorgias* 505 d). But Socrates is perfectly conscious that his mission to wake people is divine. He is constantly repeating that he is "obedient" to God (*Apology* 23 c; cf. also 30 e; 31 a; 33 c). "As you will not easily find another like me, I would advise you to spare me. I dare say that you may feel irritated *at being suddenly awakened when you are caught napping;* and you may think that if you were to strike me dead as Anytus advises, which you easily might, then you would *sleep on for the remainder of your lives,* unless God in his care of you gives you another gadfly" (*Apol.* 30, e; trans. Jowett).

We should take note of this idea that it is God who, for the love of men, sends them a Master to "awaken" them from their sleep—a sleep that is at once ignorance, forgetfulness,

12 Cf. F. Cumont, *op. cit.,* p. 450.

and "death." The motif reappears in Gnosticism, though, of course, considerably elaborated and reinterpreted. The central Gnostic myth, as we find it in the *Hymn of the Pearl,* preserved in the *Acts of Thomas,* is constructed around the theme of amnesia and *anamnesis.* A prince comes to Egypt from the East, seeking "the one pearl, which is in the midst of the sea around the loud breathing serpent." In Egypt he was made prisoner by the men of the country. He was given their food to eat and forgot his identity. "I forgot that I was a son of kings, and I served their king; and I forgot the pearl, for which my parents had sent me, and because of the burden of their oppressions I lay in a deep sleep." But his parents learned what had befallen him and sent him a letter. " 'From thy father, the king of kings, and thy mother, the mistress of the East, and from thy brother, our second (in authority), to thee our son. Call to mind that thou art a son of kings! See the slavery,—whom thou servest! Remember the pearl, for which thou wast sent to Egypt!' " The letter flew in the likeness of an eagle, alighted beside him, and became all speech. "At its voice and the sound of its rustling, I started and rose from my sleep. I took it up and kissed it, and I began and read it; and according to what was traced on my heart were the words of my letter written. I remember that I was a son of royal parents, and my noble birth asserted its nature. I remember the pearl, for which I had been sent to Egypt, and I began to charm him, the terrible loud-breathing serpent. I hushed him to sleep and lulled him into slumber, for my father's name I named over him, and I snatched away the pearl, and turned to go back to my father's house."[13]

[13] H. Leisegang, *La Gnose,* trans. by Jean Gouillard (Paris, 1951), pp. 247–248; Robert M. Grant, *Gnosticism. A Source Book of Heretical Writ-*

The *Hymn of the Pearl* has a sequel (the "luminous gar-
ment" that the prince put off when he started on his journey
to Egypt and finds again when he reaches home) which is
not directly to our purpose. We may add that the themes of
exile, captivity in a foreign country, the messenger who wakes
the prisoner and urges him to set off, are also to be found
in a short work by Suhrawardi, the *Recital of Western Exile*.[14]
We shall not here discuss the origin of the myth; it is probably Iranian. The *Hymn of the Pearl* has the value of presenting some of the most popular Gnostic motifs in a dramatic
form. Recently Hans Jonas, analyzing the specifically Gnostic
symbols and images, has stressed the importance of the
motifs of "fall, capture, forlornness, homesickness, numbness,
sleep, drunkenness."[15] This is too long a list to deal with here.
We will merely cite a few especially suggestive examples.

Turning toward matter "and burning with the desire to
experience the body," the soul forgets its identity. "She forgot
her original habitation, her true center, her eternal being."
It is in these terms that El Chātībī presents the central belief
of the Harranites.[16] According to the Gnostics, men not only
sleep but love to sleep. "Why will ye love the sleep, and
stumble with them that stumble?" asks the *Gīnza*.[17] In the

ings from the Early Christian Period (New York, 1961), pp. 116 ff. (The
English translation given is from William Wright, *Apocryphal Acts of the
Apostles* [London, 1871].) G. Widengren, "Der iranische Hintergrund
der Gnosis" (*Zeitschrift für Religions und Geistesgeschichte,* vol. IV
[1952], pp. 111 ff.), argues for the Iranian, probably Parthian, origin of
this myth.

[14] Henry Corbin, "L'Homme de Lumière dans le Soufisme Iranien"
(in the collective volume *Ombre et Lumière* [Paris, 1961], pp. 154 ff.),
with bibliographical references to his previous publications.

[15] Hans Jonas, *The Gnostic Religion* (Boston, 1958), pp. 62 ff.

[16] *Ibid.,* p. 63.

[17] Quoted by Jonas, p. 70.

Apocryphon of John it is written: "Let him who hears wake from heavy sleep."[18] The same motif recurs in Manichaean cosmogony, as transmitted to us by Theodore bar Konai: "Jesus the Luminous went down to the innocent Adam and waked him from a sleep of death that he might be delivered."[19] Ignorance and sleep are also expressed in terms of "intoxication." The *Gospel of Truth* compares the possessor of Gnosis to "one who, having been intoxicated, becomes sober and having come to himself reaffirms that which is essentially his own."[20] And the *Ginza* tells how Adam "awoke from his slumber and lifted his eyes to the place of the light."[21]

Jonas rightly remarks that, on the one hand, earthly life is defined as "forlornness," "dread," "nostalgia," and, on the other, is described as "sleep," "drunkenness," and "oblivion": "that is to say, it has assumed (if we except drunkenness) all the characteristics which a former time ascribed to the dead in the underworld."[22] The "messenger" who "wakes" man from his sleep brings him both "life" and "salvation." "I am the call of awakening from sleep in the Aeon of the night," is the beginning of a Gnostic fragment preserved by Hippolytus (*Refut.* V, 14, 1). "Waking" implies *anamnesis,* recognition of the soul's true identity, that is, re-cognition of its celestial origin. It is only after waking the man to whom he has come that the "messenger" reveals to him the promise of redemption and finally teaches him how to act in this

[18] Jean Doresse, *Les Livres secrets des Gnostiques d'Egypte* (Paris, 1958), vol. I, p. 227.

[19] F. Cumont, *Recherches sur le manichéisme I. La cosmogonie manichéenne d'après Théodore bar Khôni* (Brussels, 1908), pp. 46 ff.; J. Doresse, *op. cit.,* vol. I, pp. 235 ff.

[20] H. Jonas, *op. cit.,* p. 71.

[21] *Ibid.,* p. 74.

[22] *Ibid.,* p. 68.

world.[23] "Shake off the drunkenness in which thou hast slumbered, awake and behold me!" says a Manichaean text from Turfan.[24] And in another we find: "Awake, soul of splendour, from the slumber of drunkenness into which thou hast fallen, . . . follow me to the place of the exalted earth where thou dwelledst from the beginning."[25] A Mandaean text tells of the celestial messenger's waking Adam and continues: "I have come and will instruct thee, Adam, and release thee out of this world. Hearken and hear and be instructed, and rise up victorious to the place of light."[26] The instruction also includes the injunction not to succumb again to sleep. "Slumber not nor sleep, and forget not that which thy Lord hath charged thee."[27]

Of course, these formulas are not used only by the Gnostics. The *Epistle to the Ephesians* (5:14) contains this anonymous quotation: "Awake thou that sleepest, and arise from the dead, and Christ shall give thee light." The motif of sleep and waking recurs in Hermetic literature. We find in the *Poimandres:* "O ye people, earthborn men, who have abandoned yourselves to drunkenness and sleep and to ignorance of God—become sober! cease from your intoxication, from the enchantment of irrational sleep!"[28]

It is significant here that overcoming sleep and remaining awake for a long period is a typical initiatory ordeal. It is already found on the archaic levels of culture. Among some Australian tribes novices undergoing initiation are not allowed

---

[23] *Ibid.*, p. 23.
[24] *Ibid.*, p. 83.
[25] *Ibid.*, p. 83.
[26] *Ibid.*, p. 84.
[27] *Ibid.*, p. 84.
[28] *Corpus Hermeticum*, I, 27 f.; H. Jonas, *op. cit.*, p. 86.

to sleep for three days or are forbidden to go to bed before dawn.[29] Setting off on his quest for immortality, the Mesopotamian hero Gilgamesh comes to the island of the mythical ancestor Utnaphishtim. There he must stay awake for six days and six nights; but he does not succeed in this initiatory ordeal and so loses his chance for immortality. In a North American myth of the Orpheus-and-Eurydice type a man whose wife had just died managed to make his way down to the Underworld and find her. The Lord of the Underworld promises him that he may take his wife back to earth if he can stay awake all night. But the man falls asleep just before dawn. The Lord of the Underworld gives him another chance; and in order not to be tired the following night, the man sleeps all day. Nevertheless, he does not succeed in staying awake until dawn, and he has to return to earth alone.[30]

We see, then, that not sleeping is not merely conquering physical fatigue but is above all a proof of spiritual strength. Remaining "awake" means being fully conscious, being present in the world of the spirit. Jesus never tired of exhorting his disciples to watch (cf., for example, Matt. 24:42). And the Night of Gethsemane is made particularly tragic by the disciples' inability to stay awake with Jesus. "My soul is exceeding sorrowful, even unto death: tarry ye here, and watch with me" (Matt. 26:38). But when he came back he found them sleeping. He said to Peter: "What, could ye not watch with me one hour?" (26:40). "Watch and pray," he bids them once more. But in vain, for when he comes back he finds them "asleep again: for their eyes were heavy" (26:41–43; cf. Mark 14:34 ff.; Luke 22:46).

[29] Cf. M. Eliade, *Birth and Rebirth,* pp. 14 ff.
[30] Cf. M. Eliade, *Le Chamanisme et les techniques archaïques de l'extase,* pp. 281 ff.

This time, too, the "initiatory watch" proved to be beyond human capacity.

Gnosticism and Indian philosophy

There is not room in this short book to discuss the entire problem of Gnosticism. We set out to trace the "mythology of Forgetting and Remembering" in some higher cultures. The Gnostic texts that we have quoted stress, on the one hand, the soul's fall into Matter (Life) and the mortal "sleep" that ensues, and, on the other hand, the soul's extraterrestrial origin. The fall of the soul into matter is not the result of an earlier sin, as Greek speculation sometimes explained trans-migration. The Gnostics imply that the sin was committed by someone else.[31] Since they are Spiritual Beings of extra-terrestrial origin, the Gnostics do not admit that their home is "here," in this world. As H. C. Puech notes, the key word in the Gnostic technical language is the "other," the "alien."[32] The crowning revelation is that "though he (the Gnostic) is in the world, moves in the world, he is not of the world, he does not belong to it, but he comes and is from elsewhere."[33] The Mandaean Right-hand *Ginza* reveals to him: "Thou art not from here, thy root is not of the world" (XV, 20). And the Left-hand *Ginza* (III, 4): "Thou comest not from here, thy stock is not hence; thy place is the place of Life." And we read in the *Book of John* (p. 67): "I am a man of the *Other World*."[34]

[31] Cf. R. M. Grant, *Gnosticism and Early Christianity* (New York, 1959), p. 188, n. 16.
[32] H. C. Puech, in *Annuaire du Collège de France,* 56e année (1956), p. 194.
[33] *Ibid.,* p. 198.
[34] *Ibid.,* p. 198.

As we have seen, Indian philosophical speculation, especially Sāmkhya-Yoga, takes a similar position. The Self (*purusha*) is essentially a "stranger" and has nothing to do with the World (*prakrti*). As Isvara Krishna writes (*Sāmkhya-kārikā* 19), the Self (the Spirit) "is alone, indifferent, a mere inactive spectator" in the drama of Life and History. Indeed, he goes even further: if it is true that the cycle of trasmigration is prolonged by ignorance and "sins," the cause of the "fall of the Self" into Life, the origin of the relation (which is, however, illusory) between the Self (*purusha*) and Matter (*prakrti*), are insoluble problems, or, more precisely, insoluble in the present human condition. In any case, just as for the Gnostics, it is not an original (i.e., human) sin that precipitated the Self into the round of existences.

For the purpose of our investigation, the importance of the Gnostic myth—as also the importance of Indian philosophical speculation—lies primarily in the fact that they reinterpret man's relation to the primordial drama that brought him into being. As in the archaic religions studied in the preceding chapters, for the Gnostic too, it is essential to know—or, rather, to recollect—the drama that took place in mythical Times. But, unlike a man of the archaic societies—who, learning the myths, assumes the consequences that follow from those primordial events—the Gnostic learns the myth in order *to dissociate himself from its results*. Once waked from his mortal sleep, the Gnostic (like the disciple of Sāmkhya-Yoga) understands that he bears no responsibility for the primordial catastrophe the myth narrates for him, and that hence he has no *real* relation with Life, the World, and History.

The Gnostic, like the disciple of Sāmkhya-Yoga, has already been punished for the "sin" of *forgetting his true Self*.

The sufferings that constitute every human life vanish at the moment of waking. Waking, which is at the same time an *anamnesis,* finds expression in an indifference to History, especially to contemporary History. Only the primordial myth is important. Only the events that occurred in the past of fable are worth knowing; for, by learning them, one becomes conscious of one's true nature—and awakens. Historical events proper (for example, the Trojan War, the campaigns of Alexander the Great, the murder of Julius Caesar) have no significance since they carry no soteriological message.

Anamnesis and historiography

For the Greeks too, historical events carried no soteriological messages. Yet historiography begins in Greece, with Herodotus. Herodotus tells us why he went to the trouble of writings his *Histories:* so that the deeds of men should not be lost in the passage of time. He wishes to *preserve the memory* of what the Greeks and Barbarians did. Other historians of Antiquity will compose their works for different reasons: Thucydides, for example, to illustrate the struggle for power, a trait which he considered characteristic of human nature; Polybius to show that the whole history of the world converges toward the Roman Empire and also because the experience gained from studying History can be the best education for life; Livy in order to find in History "models for ourselves and for our country"—and so on.[35]

None of these authors—not even Herodotus, with his passionate interest in exotic Gods and theologies—composed his

[35] Cf. Karl Löwith, *Meaning in History* (Chicago, 1949), pp. 6 ff.

History in the way that the authors of the oldest historical narratives in Israel did: in order to prove the existence of a divine plan and the intervention of the Supreme God in the life of a people. This does not mean that the Greek and Roman historians were necessarily unreligious. But their religious conception had no place for the intervention of a single and personal God in History; hence they did not give historical events the religious meaning they had for the Jews. Then too, for the Greeks History was only one aspect of the cosmic process conditioned by the law of becoming. Like every cosmic phenomenon, History showed that human societies are born, develop, decay, and perish. This is why History could not be an object of knowledge. Yet historiography was useful, for it illustrated the process of eternal becoming in the life of nations, and especially because it preserved the memory of the exploits of various peoples and the names and adventures of outstanding personages.

It is not within the scope of this essay to examine the various philosophies of History, from Augustine and Gioacchino da Fiore to Vico, Hegel, Marx, and the contemporary historicists. All these systems set out to discover the *meaning* and *direction* of universal History. But that is not our problem. What is of interest to our investigation is not the meaning that *History* may have but *historiography* itself—in other words, the *endeavor to preserve the memory* of contemporary events and the desire to know the past of humanity as accurately as possible.

Such a curiosity has developed progressively ever since the Middle Ages and especially since the Renaissance. Certainly, in the time of the Renaissance ancient history was studied primarily for the sake of finding models for the behavior of

the "perfect man." Indeed we could say that, by supplying
exemplary models for civic and moral life, Livy and Plutarch
played the same role in the education of the European elites
as myths did in traditional societies. But it is from the nineteenth century on that historiography has been led to play
a role of primary importance. It seems as if Western culture
were making a prodigious effort of historiographic *anamnesis*.
It seeks to discover, "awaken," and repossess the pasts of the
most exotic and the most peripheral societies, from the prehistoric Near East to "primitive" cultures on the verge of
extinction. The goal is no less than to revive the *entire past
of humanity*. We are witnessing a vertiginous widening of the
historical horizon.

This is one of the few encouraging syndromes of the modern
world. Western cultural provincialism—which began history
with Egypt, literature with Homer, and philosophy with
Thales—is being rapidly outmoded. But that is not all: through
this historiographic *anamnesis* man enters deep into himself.
If we succeed in understanding a contemporary Australian,
or his homologue, a paleolithic hunter, we have succeeded
in "awakening" in the depths of our being the existential
situation and the resultant behavior of a prehistoric humanity.
It is not a matter of a mere "external" knowledge, as when
we learn the name of the capital of a country or the date of
the fall of Constantinople. A true historiographic *anamnesis*
finds expression in the discovery of our solidarity with these
vanished or peripheral peoples. We have a genuine recovery
of the past, even of the "primordial" past revealed by un-
covering prehistoric sites or by ethnological investigations. In
these last two cases, we are confronted by "forms of life,"

behavior patterns, types of culture—in short, by the structures —of archaic existence.

For millenniums man worked ritually and thought mythically concerning the analogies between the macrocosm and the microcosm. It was one of the possible ways of "opening oneself" to the World and thereby sharing in the sacrality of the Cosmos. Since the Renaissance, since the Universe proved to be infinite, this cosmic dimension that man ritually added to his life is denied to us. It was to be expected that modern man, fallen under the domination of Time and obsessed by his own historicity, should try to "open himself" to the World by acquiring a new dimension in the vastness of the temporal realm. Unconsciously, he defends himself against the pressure of contemporary history by a historiographic *anamnesis* that opens perspectives he could not possibly suspect if, following Hegel's example, he had confined himself to "communing with the Universal Spirit" while reading his newspaper every morning.

To be sure, this is no new discovery: from Antiquity on, man consoled himself for the terror of History by reading the historians of past times. But in the case of modern man there is something more. His historiographic horizon being as wide as it has become, he is able, through *anamnesis,* to discover cultures that, though they "sabotaged History," were prodigiously creative. How vitally will it affect the life of a modern Westerner when he learns, for example, that though the Indian peninsula was invaded and occupied by Alexander the Great and though his conquest had a capital influence on its history, India has not even remembered the great conqueror's name? Like other traditional cultures, India is concerned with exemplary models and paradigmatic events, not with the particular and the individual.

The historiographic *anamnesis* of the Western world is only beginning. At least several generations must pass before its cultural repercussions can be gauged. But we may say that, though on a different plane, this *anamnesis* continues the religious evaluation of memory and forgetfulness. To be sure, neither myths nor religious practices are any longer involved. But there is this common element: the importance of precise and total recollection of the past. In the traditional societies it is recollection of *mythical events;* in the modern West it is recollection of *all that took place in historical Time.* The difference is too obvious to require definition. But both types of *anamnesis* project man out of his "historical moment." And true historiographic *anamnesis* opens, too, on a primordial Time, the Time in which men established their cultural behavior patterns, even though believing that they were revealed to them by Supernatural Beings.

VIII.

Greatness and Decadence of Myths

Keeping the World open

ON THE ARCHAIC levels of culture religion maintains the "opening" toward a superhuman world, the world of axiological values. These values are "transcendent," in the sense that they are held to be revealed by Divine Beings or mythical Ancestors. Hence they constitute absolute values, paradigms for all human activities. As we have seen, these models are conveyed by myths. Myths are the most general and effective means of awakening and maintaining consciousness of another world, a beyond, whether it be the divine world or the world of the Ancestors. This "other world" represents a superhuman, "transcendent" plane, the plane of *absolute realities*. It is the experience of the sacred—that is, an encounter with a transhuman reality—which gives birth to the idea that something *really exists,* that hence there are absolute values capable of guiding man and giving a meaning to human existence. It is, then, through the experience of the sacred that the ideas of *reality, truth,* and *significance* first dawn, to be later elaborated and systematized by metaphysical speculations.

The apodictic value of myth is periodically reconfirmed by the rituals. Recollection and re-enactment of the primordial event help "primitive" man to distinguish and hold to the *real.* By virtue of the continual repetition of a paradigmatic act, something shows itself to be *fixed* and *enduring* in the universal flux. This periodic reiteration of what was done *in illo tempore* makes it inescapably certain that something *exists absolutely.* This "something" is "sacred," that is, transhuman and transmundane, but it is accessible to human experience. "Reality" unveils itself and admits of being constructed from a "transcendent" level, but this "transcendence" can be ritually experienced and finally becomes an integral part of human life.

This "transcendent" world of the Gods, the Heroes, and the mythical Ancestors is accessible because archaic man does not accept the irreversibility of Time. As we have repeatedly seen, ritual abolishes profane, chronological Time and recovers the sacred Time of myth. Man becomes contemporary with the exploits that the Gods performed *in illo tempore.* On the one hand, this revolt against the irreversibility of Time helps man to "construct reality"; on the other, it frees him from the weight of dead Time, assures him that he is able to abolish the past, to begin his life anew, and to re-create his World.

The imitation of the paradigmatic acts of the Gods, the Heroes, and the mythical Ancestors does not produce an "eternal repetition of the same thing," a total cultural immobility. Ethnology knows of no single people that has not changed in the course of time, that has not had a "history." At first sight the man of the archaic societies seems only to repeat the same archetypal act forever. But actually he is tirelessly conquering the World, organizing it, transforming the landscape of nature into a cultural milieu. For by virtue of the exemplary model revealed by the cosmogonic myth, man, too, becomes creative. Though the myths, by presenting themselves as sacrosanct models, would seem to paralyze human initiative, actually they stimulate man to create, they are constantly opening new perspectives to his inventiveness.

Myth assures man that what he is about to do *has already been done,* in other words, it helps him to overcome doubts as to the result of his undertaking. There is no reason to hesitate before setting out on a sea voyage, because the mythical Hero has already made it in a fabulous Time. All that is needed is to follow his example. Similarly, there is no reason to fear settling in an unknown, wild territory, because one knows what one has to do. One has merely to repeat the cosmogonic ritual, whereupon the unknown territory (= "Chaos") is transformed into "Cosmos," becomes an *imago mundi* and hence a ritually legitimized "habitation." The existence of an exemplary model does not fetter creative innovation. The possibilities for applying the mythical model are endless.

The man of the societies in which myth is a living thing lives in a World that, though "in cipher" and mysterious, is "open." The World "speaks" to man, and to understand its language he needs only to know the myths and decipher the symbols. Through the myths and symbols of the Moon man grasps the mysterious solidarity among temporality, birth, death and resurrection, sexuality, fertility, rain, vegetation, and so on. The World is no longer an opaque mass of objects arbitrarily thrown together, it is a living Cosmos, articulated and meaningful. In the last analysis, *the World reveals itself as language*. It speaks to man through its own mode of being, through its structures and its rhythms.

That the World exists is due to a divine act of creation.

its structures and its rhythms are the product of events that
took place at the beginning of Time. The Moon has its mythical history, but so have the Sun and the Waters, plants and
animals. Every significant cosmic object has a "history." This
is as much as to say that it can "speak" to man. Because it
"speaks" of itself—above all of its "origin," the primordial
event in consequence of which it came into being—the object
becomes *real* and *significant*. It is no longer something "unknown," that is, an opaque object, inapprehensible, meaning-
less, and in the last analysis "unreal." It shares in the same
"World" as man.

This co-participation not only makes the World "familiar"
and intelligible, it makes it transparent. Through the objects
of this present World one perceives traces of the Beings and
powers of another world. This is why we said earlier that
for archaic man the World is at once "open" and mysterious.
Speaking of itself, the World refers back to its authors and
guardians and tells its "history." The result is that, on the one
hand, man does not find himself existing in an inert, opaque
world; on the other, deciphering the World's language, he is
confronted by mystery. For "Nature" at once unveils and
"camouflages" the "supernatural"; and this, for archaic man,
constitutes the basic and unfathomable mystery of the World.
The myths reveal all that has taken place, from the cosmogony
to the establishment of socio-cultural institutions. But these
revelations do not constitute "knowledge" in the strict sense,
they do not exhaust the mystery of cosmic and human realities.
By learning their origin myth, one becomes able to control
various cosmic realities (for example, fire, harvests, snakes,
etc.); but this does not mean that one has transformed them

into "objects of knowledge." These realities still keep their original ontological condition.

Man and the World

In such a World man does not feel shut up in his own mode of existence. He too is "open." He achieves communication with the World because he uses the same language —symbol. If the World speaks to him through its heavenly bodies, its plants and animals, its rivers and rocks, its seasons and nights, man answers it by his dreams and his imaginative life, by his Ancestors or his totems (at once "Nature," supernatural, and human beings), by his ability to die and return to life ritually in initiation ceremonies (like the Moon and vegetation), by his power to incarnate a spirit by putting on a mask, and so on. If for archaic man the World is transparent, he feels that he too is "looked at" and understood by the World. It is not only the game animal that looks at him and understands him (very often the animal allows itself to be caught because it knows the man is hungry), but also the rock or the tree or the river. Each has its "history" to tell him, advice to give him.

Even while he knows that he is a human being, and accepts himself as such, the man of the archaic societies knows, too, that he is something more. He knows, for example, that his Ancestor was an animal, or that he can die and come back to life (initiation, shamanic trance), that he can influence the crops by his orgies (in other words, that he can do to his wife as the Sky does to the Earth, or that he can play the role of the hoe and she that of the furrow). In more complex cultures man knows that his breaths are Winds, that his bones are like mountains, that a fire burns in his belly, that his navel can become a "Center of the World," and so on.

But it would be wrong to suppose that this "openness" to the World has its counterpart in a bucolic conception of life. The myths of the "primitives" and the rituals that stem from them show us no archaic Arcadia. By assuming the responsibility for making the vegetable world prosper, the paleo-cultivators also accepted torturing victims for the benefit of crops, sexual orgies, cannibalism, head-hunting. This is a tragic conception of life, resulting from the religious valuation of torture and violent death. A myth like that of Hainuwele, and the entire socio-religious complex that it articulates and justifies, obliges man to assume his condition of a sexed and mortal being, condemned to kill and to work in order to feed himself. The vegetable and animal world "speaks" to him of its origin, that is, in the last analysis, of Hainuwele; and the paleo-cultivator understands its language and, in so doing, finds a religious meaning in everything around him and in everything that he does. But this obliges him to accept cruelty and murder as integral to his mode of being. To be sure, cruelty, torture, and murder are not forms of conduct peculiar only to "primitives." They are found throughout the course of History, sometimes to a paroxysmic degree never reached in the archaic societies. The difference lies primarily in the fact that, for primitives, this violent behavior has a religious value and is imitated from transhuman models. This conception survived quite late into History; Genghis Khan's mass exterminations, for example, still claimed to have a religious justification.

Myth, in itself, is not a guarantee of "goodness" or morality.

Its function is to reveal models and, in so doing, to give a meaning to the World and to human life. This is why its role in the constitution of man is immense. It is through myth, as we said before, that the ideas of *reality, value, transcendence* slowly dawn. Through myth, the World can be apprehended as a perfectly articulated, intelligible, and significant Cosmos. In telling how things were made, myth reveals by whom and why they were made and under what circumstances. All these "revelations" involve man more or less directly, for they make up a Sacred History.

Imagination and creativity

In short, myths are a constant reminder that grandiose events took place on Earth and that this "glorious past" is partly recoverable. The imitation of paradigmatic acts also has a positive aspect: the rite forces man to transcend his limitations, obliges him to take his place with the Gods and the mythical Heroes so that he can perform their deeds. Directly or indirectly, myth "elevates" man. This becomes even clearer if we bear in mind that in archaic societies recitation of the mythological traditions remains the prerogative of a few individuals. In some societies the reciters are recruited among the shamans and medicine men or among members of the secret societies. In any case, he who recites the myths has had to prove his vocation and receive instruction from the old masters. He is always someone notable either for his mnemonic capacity or for his imagination or literary talent.

The recitation is not necessarily stereotyped. Sometimes the variants depart considerably from the prototype. Obviously, the investigations conducted in our day by ethnologists and folklorists lay no claim to unveiling the process of mythological creation. The variants of a myth or of a folklore theme can be and have been recorded, but not the invention of a new myth. Recorded myths are always more or less marked modifications of a pre-existing text.

But these researches have brought out the role of creative individuals in the elaboration and transmission of myths. In all probability this role was even greater in the past, when what is today called "poetic creativity" was bound up with and dependent upon an ecstatic experience. Now, it is possible to divine the "sources of inspiration" for such a creative personality in an archaic society: they are "crises," "encounters," "revelations," that is, privileged religious experiences, accompanied and enriched by a host of particularly living and dramatic images and scenarios. It is the specialists in ecstasy, the familiars of fantastic universes, who nourish, increase, and elaborate the traditional mythological motifs.

In the last analysis, it is a creativity on the plane of the religious imagination that renews traditional mythological material. This means that the role of creative personalities must have been greater than is suspected. The different specialists in the sacred, from shamans to bards, finally succeeded in imposing at least some of their imaginary visions on the respective collectivities. To be sure, the "success" of any such vision depended on the already existing schemas: a vision in basic contradiction to the traditional images and scenarios was not likely to win easy acceptance. But the role of medicine men, shamans, and old masters in the religious life of the archaic societies is well known. They are all individuals variously specializing in ecstatic experiences. The relations between the traditional schemas and the new individual revaluations are not rigid: under the impact of a strong religious personality the traditional pattern finally yields to change.

All this is as much as to say that privileged religious experiences, when they are communicated through a sufficiently impressive and fanciful scenario, succeed in imposing models or sources of inspiration on the whole community. In the last analysis, in the archaic societies as everywhere else, culture arises and is renewed through the creative experiences of a few individuals. But since archaic culture gravitates around myths, and these are constantly being studied and given new, more profound interpretations by the specialists in the sacred, it follows that the society as a whole is led toward the values and meanings discovered and conveyed by these few individuals. It is in this way that myth helps man to transcend his own limitations and conditions and stimulates him to rise to "where the greatest are."

Homer

An entire study could well be devoted to the relations between the great religious personalities, especially the reformers and prophets, and the traditional mythological schemas. The messianic and millennialist movements among the peoples of the former colonies represent a practically unlimited field for research. It would be possible to reconstruct, at least in part, the impact of Zarathustra on Iranian mythology or that of the Buddha on the traditional mythologies of India. As for Judaism, the great "demythicization" performed by the prophets has long been known.

The scope of this short book does not allow us to discuss these problems with the attention they deserve. We prefer to dwell for a little on Greek mythology—less on what it represents in itself than on some of its relations to Christianity.

The problem of Greek myth is one to give the investigator pause. Only in Greece did myth inspire and guide not only epic poetry, tragedy, and comedy but also the plastic arts; on the other hand, only in the culture of Greece was myth submitted to a long and penetrating analysis, from which it emerged radically "demystified." The rise of Ionian rationalism coincides with a more and more damaging criticism of the "classic" mythology as it found expression in the works of Homer and Hesiod. If in every European language the word "myth" denotes a "fiction," it is because the Greeks proclaimed it to be such twenty-five centuries ago.

Willy-nilly, every attempt to interpret Greek myth, at least within a culture of the Western type, is in some sort conditioned by the critique of the Greek rationalists. As we shall see in a moment, this critique was seldom directed against what we have called "mythical thought" or the resultant type of behavior. The criticisms were aimed primarily at the doings of the Gods as narrated by Homer and Hesiod. We may well wonder what a Xenophanes would have thought of the Polynesian cosmogonic myth or of a speculative Vedic myth such as that in *Rig Veda* X, 129. Obviously, we cannot know. But it is important to emphasize the fact that the target of the rationalists' attacks was primarily the adventures and arbitrary decisions of the Gods, their capricious and unjust behavior, their "immorality." And the main critique was made in the name of an increasingly higher idea of God: a true God could not be unjust, immoral, jealous, vindictive, ignorant, and the like. The same critique was later renewed

and exacerbated by the Christian apologists. This thesis—
more particularly the objection that the divine myths as presented by the poets cannot be true—triumphed, at first among
the Greek intellectual elites and finally, after the victory of
Christianity, everywhere in the Greco-Roman world.

But it is only justice to remember that Homer was neither
a theologian nor a mythographer. In other words, he laid no
claim to presenting the whole body of Greek religion and
mythology systematically and exhaustively. Though, as Plato
put it, Homer had educated all Greece, he had composed his
poems for a specific audience: the members of a military
and feudal aristocracy. His literary genius had exercised a
fascination never equaled by any other author; hence his
works greatly contributed toward unifying and articulating
Greek culture. But since he was not writing a treatise on
mythology, he did not record all the mythological themes
that were in circulation in the Greek world. Then too, he
avoided evoking religious or mythological conceptions that
were either foreign to his essentially patriarchal and military
auditors or in which they took little interest. Concerning all
that could be called the nocturnal, chthonian, funereal side
of Greek religion and mythology, Homer says next to nothing.
The importance of the religious ideas of sexuality and fecundity, of death, and the life after death has been made known
to us by late writers and archaeological excavations. It was,
then, this Homeric conception of the Gods and their myths
that imposed itself throughout the world and that was finally
fixed, as if in a timeless universe of archetypes, by the great
artists of the classical period. We need not dwell on its greatness, its nobility, and its role in forming the Western spirit.

One need only reread Walter Otto's *Die Götter Griechenlands* in order to commune with this luminous world of "Perfect Forms."

But the fact that Homer's genius and classical art gave a matchless glory to this divine world does not necessarily imply that everything omitted from it was dark, obscure, inferior, or mediocre. There was Dionysus, for example, without whom Greece is inconceivable and to whom Homer's only reference is an allusion to an incident of his childhood. Then too, mythological fragments preserved by historians and antiquarians introduce us to a spiritual world that is not lacking in greatness. These non-Homeric and, in general, non-"classic" mythologies were apt to be "popular." They did not suffer the erosion of rationalistic criticism and, in all probability, survived on the margin of literate culture for many centuries. It is not impossible that vestiges of these popular mythologies still subsist, camouflaged and "Christianized," in the Greek and Mediterranean beliefs of our time. We shall return to this problem.

Theogony and genealogy

Hesiod addressed a different audience. That is why he narrates myths that are passed over in silence or barely alluded to in the Homeric poems. For example, he is the first to tell of Prometheus. But he could not know that the central myth of Prometheus was based on a misapprehension, or, more precisely, on its primordial religious meaning having been "forgotten." The fact is that Zeus takes vengeance on Prometheus because the latter, summoned to preside over the sharing out of the first sacrificial victim, had covered the bones with a layer of fat, and the flesh and entrails with the stomach. Attracted by the fat, Zeus had chosen the poorer share for the Gods, leaving the flesh and entrails to men (*Theogony,* 534 ff.). Now, Karl Meuli[1] has compared this Olympian sacrifice with the rituals of the archaic North Asian hunters; the latter venerate their celestial Supreme Beings by offering them the animal's bones and head. The same ritual custom has survived among the pastoral peoples of Central Asia. What, during an archaic stage of culture, had been considered the most perfect homage to a celestial God had in Greece become the consummate example of cheating, the crime of lèse-majesté against Zeus, the supreme God. We do not know when this shift of the original ritual meaning occurred, nor how Prometheus came to be accused of the crime. We have given the example only to show that Hesiod cites extremely archaic myths, rooted deep in pre-History; but these myths had undergone a long process of transformation and modification before the poet recorded them.

Obviously, Hesiod does not confine himself to recording myths. He systematizes them and, by so doing, already introduces a rational principle into these creations of mythical thought. Hesiod understands the genealogy of the Gods as a successive series of procreations. For him, procreation is the ideal way of coming into existence. W. Jaeger has rightly brought out the rational nature of this conception, in which mythical thought is given articulation by causal thought.[2] Hesiod's idea that Eros was the first God to appear after Chaos

[1] Karl Meuli, "Griechische Opferbräuche," *Phyllobolia für Peter Von der Mühl* (Basel, 1946), pp. 185–288.

[2] Werner Jaeger, *Paideia: The Ideals of Greek Culture* (2nd ed., New York, 1945), vol. I, pp. 65 ff.; *id., The Theology of the Early Greek Philosophers* (Oxford, 1947), p. 12.

and Earth (*Theogony,* 116 ff.) was later developed by Par-
menides and Empedocles.[3] Plato, in the *Banquet* (178 b), has
emphasized the importance of this conception for Greek
philosophy.

The rationalists and myth

We cannot here even summarize the long process of erosion
by which the Homeric myths and Gods were finally emptied
of their original meanings. If we are to believe Herodotus
(I, 32), Solon already said that "the deity is full of envy
and instability." In any case, the earliest Milesian philosophers
refused to see the Figure of the true divinity in Homer's
descriptions. When Thales affirmed that "every thing is full
of gods" (A 22), he was revolting against the Homeric idea
that the Gods inhabited only certain regions of the Cosmos.
Anaximander attempts to present a total conception of the
Universe, without gods and without myths. As for Xenophanes
(born *ca.* 565), he does not hesitate to attack the Homeric
pantheon openly. He refuses to believe that God moves about
from place to place, as Homer tells (B 26). He rejects the immortality of the Gods as described by Homer and Hesiod:
". . . Homer and Hesiod say that the gods do all manner
of things which men would consider disgraceful: adultery,
stealing, deceiving each other" (B 11, B 12).[4] Nor will he
accept the idea of divine procreation: ". . . But mortals consider that the gods are born, and that they have clothes and
speech and bodies like their own" (B 14).[5] He especially

[3] W. Jaeger, *The Theology of the Early Greek Philosophers,* p. 14.
[4] Trans. by Jaeger, *The Theology of the Early Greek Philosophers,* p.
47.
[5] Trans. by G. S. Kirk and J. E. Raven, *The Presocratic Philosophers*

criticizes the anthropomorphism of the Gods: "But if cattle and horses or lions had hands, or were able to draw with their hands and do the works that men can do, horses would draw the forms of gods like horses, and cattle like cattle, and they would make their bodies such as they each had themselves" (B 15).[6] For Xenophanes, "One god is the highest among gods and men; in neither his form nor his thought is he like unto mortals" (B 23, trans. W. Jaeger).

In these critiques of "classical" mythology we can see an effort to free the concept of divinity from the anthropomorphic expressions of the poets. Even a profoundly religious author like Pindar rejects the "incredible" myths (*I Olympic,* 28 ff.). Euripides' conception of God had been wholly influenced by Xenophanes' critique. In Thucydides' day the adjective *mythodes* meant "fabulous and unauthenticated," in contrast to every kind of truth or reality.[7] When Plato (*Republic,* 378 ff.) blamed the poets for the way in which they had presented the Gods, he was probably addressing an audience that was already convinced.

The criticism of mythological traditions was almost pedantically elaborated by the Alexandrian rhetoricians. As we shall see, the Christian apologists patterned themselves on these authors when they in turn were called on to deal with the problem of distinguishing the historical elements in the Gos-

---

(Cambridge, Mass., 1957), p. 168; cf. also Kathleen Freeman, *Ancilla to the Pre-Socratic Philosophers* (Cambridge, Mass., 1948), p. 22. Documents and bibliographies on the Milesians in Pierre Maxime Schuhl, *Essai sur la formation de la pensée grecque* (2nd ed., Paris, 1949), pp. 163 ff., and in Kathleen Freeman, *The Pre-Socratic Philosophers. A Companion to Diels,* FRAGMENTE DER VORSOKRATIKER (Oxford, 1946), pp. 49 ff.

[6] Trans. Kirk and Raven, *op. cit.,* p. 169.

[7] Cf. Thucydides, *History,* i. 21; W. Jaeger, *The Theology of the Early Greek Philosophers,* pp. 19, 197–98.

pels. The Alexandrian Aelius Theon (*ca.* second century A.D.) discourses at length on the arguments by which it is possible to demonstrate the "incredibility" of a myth or a historical narrative, and he illustrates his methods by a critical analysis of the myth of Medea. Theon considers that a mother could not kill her own children. In addition, the act is "incredible" because Medea could not have slaughtered her children in the very city (Corinth) in which their father Jason was living. Then again, the way in which the crime was committed is improbable: Medea would have tried to hide her guilt and, being a witch, she would have used poison instead of the sword. Finally the alleged reason for her act is highly improbable: anger against her husband could not have driven her to cut the throats of their children, which were at the same time her own; in doing so, the person she hurt most was herself, since women are more prone to emotions than men.[8]

Allegorization and euhemerism

This is more than a devastating critique of the myth; it is a critique of any imaginary world, leveled in the name of a simplistic psychology and an elementary rationalism. Nevertheless, the mythology of Homer and Hesiod continued to interest the elites in all parts of the Hellenistic world. But the myths were no longer taken literally: what was now sought was their "hidden meanings" (*hyponoiai;* the term *"allegoria"* was used later). Theagenes of Rhegium (fl. *ca.* 525) had

---

[8] Aelius Theon, *Progymnasmata* (94, 12–32), summarized by Robert M. Grant, *The Earliest Lives of Jesus* (New York, 1961), pp. 41–42; cf. also *ibid.,* p. 120 ff.

already suggested that the names of the Gods in Homer represented either the human faculties or the natural elements. But it was especially the Stoics who developed the allegorical interpretation of Homeric mythology and, in general, of all religious traditions. Chrysippus reduced the Greek Gods to physical or ethical principles. In the *Quaestiones Homericae* of Heraclitus (first century A.D.) there is a whole series of allegorical interpretations: for example, when the myth tells that Zeus bound Hera, the episode really signifies that the ether is the limit of the air, and so on. The allegorical method was applied by Philo to decipher and illustrate the "enigmas" of the Old Testament. As we shall see later, allegorical interpretation of a sort, particularly typology (that is, the correspondence between the two Testaments), was freely used by the Fathers, especially Origen.

Some scholars hold that allegory was never very popular in Greece and had more success in Alexandria and Rome. It is none the less true that various allegorical interpretations "saved" Homer and Hesiod in the eyes of the Greek elites and made it possible for the Homeric Gods to retain a high cultural value. The rescue of the Homeric pantheon and mythology is not the work of the allegorical method alone. At the beginning of the third century B.C. Euhemerus published a romance in the form of a philosophical voyage, *Sacred Writing (Hyera anagraphe)*, the success of which was great and immediate. Ennius translated it into Latin; indeed, it was the first Greek text to be translated. Euhemerus believed that he had discovered the origin of the Gods: they were ancient kings deified. Here was another "rational" way to preserve the Gods of Homer. They now had a "reality": it was historical (or, more precisely, prehistorical); their myths represented the confused memory or an imaginative transfiguration of the exploits of the primitive kings.

This allegorizing in reverse had wide repercussions, undreamed of by Euhemerus and Ennius, and even by Lactantius and other Christian apologists when the latter took their stand on Euhemerus to demonstrate the humanity, and hence the unreality, of the Greek Gods. By force of allegorical interpretation and euhemerism, and more especially of the fact that all literature and all plastic art had developed around the divine and heroic myths, the Greek Gods and Heroes did not sink into oblivion after the long process of "demythicization" or even after the triumph of Christianity.

On the contrary, as Jean Seznec has shown in his excellent book, *The Survival of the Pagan Gods,* the euhemerized Greek Gods survived all through the Middle Ages, though they had shed their classic forms and were camouflaged under the most unexpected disguises. The "rediscovery" of the Renaissance consists primarily in the restoration of the pure, "classic" forms.[9] And in fact it was toward the end of the Renaissance that the Western world realized there was no longer any possibility of combining Greco-Latin "paganism" with Christianity; whereas in the Middle Ages antiquity was not regarded as a "distinct historical milieu, as a period that had run its course."[10]

So it is that a secularized mythology and a euhemerized pantheon managed to survive and, from the time of the Renaissance, to become a subject of scientific investigation—precisely because dying antiquity no longer believed in Homer's

[9] Jean Seznec, *The Survival of the Pagan Gods. The Mythological Tradition and its place in Renaissance Humanism and Art* (New York, 1953), pp. 320 ff.

[10] *Ibid.,* p. 322.

Gods or in the original meaning of their myths. All this mythological heritage could be accepted and assimilated by Christianity because it no longer carried living religious values. It had become a "cultural treasure." In the last analysis, the classical heritage was "saved" by the poets, the artists, and the philosophers. From the end of antiquity—when no cultivated person any longer took them literally—the Gods and their myths were conveyed to the Renaissance and the seventeenth century by *works,* by creations of literature and art.

Written documents and oral traditions

Through *culture,* a desacralized religious universe and a demythicized mythology formed and nourished Western civilization—that is, the only civilization that has succeeded in becoming exemplary. There is more here than a triumph of *logos* over *mythos.* The victory is that of *the book* over oral tradition, of the document—especially of the written document—over a living experience whose only means of expression were preliterary. A great many antique written texts and works of art have perished. Yet enough remain to enable the admirable Mediterranean civilization to be reconstructed in outline. This is not the case with the preliterary forms of culture, in Greece as well as in ancient Europe. We know very little about the popular religions and mythologies of the Mediterranean, and that little we owe to the monuments and a few written documents. In some cases—the Eleusinian mysteries, for example—the scantness of our information is explained by the fact that initiatory secrecy was well kept. In other cases what we know of one or another popular belief or cult is due to some lucky chance. To give only one example, if Pausanias had not recorded his personal experience at the oracle of Trophonius in Lebadeia (IX, 39), we should have had to make do with the few vague allusions in Hesiod, Euripides, and Aristophanes. In other words, we should not have suspected the significance and importance of that religious center.

The "classic" Greek myths already represent the triumph of the literary *work* over religious *belief*. Not a single Greek myth has come down to us in its cult context. We know the myths as literary and artistic "documents," not as the sources, or expressions, of a religious experience bound up with a rite. The whole *living* and popular side of Greek religion escapes us, precisely because it was not systematically expressed in writing.

We must not judge the vitality of Greek religious feeling and practice solely by the degree to which the Olympian myths and cults found adherents. Criticism of the Homeric myths did not necessarily imply rationalism or atheism. The fact that the *classic forms* of mythical thought had been "compromised" by the rationalists' criticism does not mean that all mythical thought was discarded. The intellectual elites had discovered other mythologies able to justify and articulate new religious concepts. On the one hand, there were the Mystery religions, from Eleusis and the Orphico-Pythagorean brotherhoods to the Greco-Oriental mysteries that were so popular in Imperial Rome and the provinces. In addition, there were what could be called the mythologies of the soul, the soteriologies elaborated by the Neo-Pythagoreans, the Neo-Platonists, and the Gnostics. To all this we must add the spread of solar mythologies and cults, the astral and funerary mythologies, as well as all kinds of popular "superstitions" and "minor mythologies."

We have cited these few facts to forestall any assumption that the "demythicization" of Homer and the classic religion had afflicted the Mediterranean world with a religious vacuum, had left a void into which Christianity had moved almost unopposed. Actually, Christianity clashed with several types of religious expression. It was not the allegorized and euhemerized "classic" religion and mythology that represented the real resistance; their power was predominantly political and cultural; the city, the state, the Empire, together with the prestige of the incomparable Greco-Roman culture, constituted an imposing edifice. But from the point of view of living religion, the edifice was shaky, ready to crash to ruin under the impact of a genuine religious experience.

The real resistance to Christianity was found in the Mystery religions and the soteriologies (which pursued the salvation of the individual and ignored or scorned the forms of the civil religion) and especially in the popular *living* religions and mythologies of the Empire. On these religions we have even less information than we have on Greek and Mediterranean popular religion. We know something about Zalmoxis of the Getae because Herodotus had brought back a few facts about him from the Greeks of the Hellespont. Except for this, we should have had to make do with mere references, as in the case of other Thracian divinities of the Balkans— Darzales, Bendis, Kotys, etc. Whenever we have more detailed information about the pre-Christian religions of Europe, we are made aware of their richness and complexity. But since in their pagan days these peoples produced no *books,* we shall never have a thorough knowledge of their original religions and mythologies.

Yet they represented a religious life and a mythology powerful enough to resist ten centuries of Christianity and countless offensives on the part of ecclesiastical authorities. This religion was cosmic in structure, and we shall see that in the end it was tolerated and assimilated by the Church. In fact, rural Christianity, especially in Southern and Southeastern Europe, has a cosmic dimension.

So we may conclude that Greek religion and mythology, radically secularized and demythicized, survived in European *culture,* for the very reason that they had been expressed by literary and artistic masterpieces. Whereas the popular religions and mythologies, the only *living* pagan forms when Christianity triumphed (but about which we know almost nothing, since they were not expressed in writing), survived in Christianized form in the traditions of the various rural populations. Since this rural religion was essentially agricultural in structure, with roots going back to the Neolithic Age, in all probability European religious folklore still preserves a prehistoric heritage.

But these survivals of archaic myths and religious attitudes and practices, although representing an important spiritual phenomenon, had very little effect on the cultural plane. The revolution brought about by writing was irreversible. Henceforth the history of culture will consider only archaeological documents and written texts. A people without *this* kind of documents is considered a people without history. Popular creations and oral traditions will be granted value only very late, in the period of German Romanticism; the interest in them is already antiquarian. The popular creations in which mythical behavior and the mythical universe still survive have sometimes served as the source of inspiration for a few great European artists. But such popular creations have never played an important role in culture. They have ended by being regarded as "documents," and as such have tempted the curiosity of certain specialists. To interest a modern man, this *oral* traditional heritage has to be presented in the form of a *book*. . . .

IX.

Survivals and Camouflages of Myths

Christianity and mythology

THE RELATIONS between Christianity and mythical thought can hardly be presented in a few pages. For the fact is that their relations raise several quite separate problems. First of all, there is the equivocal use of the term "myth." The earliest Christian theologians took the word in the sense that had become current some centuries earlier in the Greco-Roman world, i.e., "fable, fiction, lie." They therefore refused to see a "mythical" figure in Jesus and a "myth" in the Messianic drama. From the second century on, Christian theologians had to defend the historicity of Jesus against the Docetists and the Gnostics as well as against the pagan philosophers. We shall presently see the arguments they employed to support their thesis and the difficulties they had to meet.

The second problem is in some measure bound up with the first. It does not impugn the historicity of Jesus but questions the validity of the literary documents that illustrate it. Origen was already aware how difficult it is to prove a historical event with incontrovertible documents. In our day a Rudolf Bultmann, though he does not doubt the historical existence of Jesus, insists that we can know nothing about his life and character. This methodological position assumes that the

Gospels and other primitive documents are full of "mythological elements" (taking myth, of course, to mean "what cannot exist"). It is beyond doubt that "mythological elements" abound in the Gospels. In addition, symbols, figures, and rituals of Jewish or Mediterranean origin were early assimilated by Christianity. We shall later see the significance of this twofold process of "Judaization" and "paganization" of primitive Christianity.

We may add for the moment that the vast number of symbols and elements that Christianity shares with solar cults and Mystery religions has prompted some scholars to deny the historicity of Jesus. They have, for example, taken the position opposite to Bultmann's. Instead of postulating, at the beginning of Christianity, a historical person of whom we can know nothing because of the "mythology" with which he was soon overlaid, these scholars have postulated a "myth" that was imperfectly "historicized" by the earliest generations of Christians. To mention only the moderns, from Arthur Drews (1909) and Peter Jensen (1906, 1909) to P. L. Couchoud (1924) scholars of sundry orientations and sundry degrees of competence have laboriously attempted to reconstruct the "original myth" which they hold to have given birth to the figure of Christ and finally to Christianity. This "original myth," be it said, varies from author to author. A fascinating study could be made of these at once scholarly and daring reconstructions. They betray a certain nostalgia in modern man for the "primordially mythical." (In the case of P. L. Couchoud the exaltation of the nonhistoricity of myth at the expense of the poverty of the historically concrete is glaringly obvious.) But none of these nonhistorical hypotheses has been accepted by the specialists.

Finally there is a third problem that arises when one studies the relations between mythical thought and Christianity. It can be stated as follows: If Christians have refused to see in their religion the desacralized *mythos* of the Hellenistic period, what is the situation of Christianity in respect to the *living myth,* as known in the archaic and traditional societies? We shall see that Christianity as understood and practiced during the nearly two thousand years of its history cannot be completely separated from mythical thinking.

History and "enigmas" in the Gospels

Let us now see how the Fathers attempted to defend the historicity of Jesus both against pagan unbelievers and against "heretics." Faced with the problem of presenting the authentic life of Jesus, that is, his life as it was known and orally transmitted by the Apostles, the theologians of the primitive Church found themselves confronting a certain number of texts and oral traditions circulating in different milieux. The Fathers displayed both critical faculty and "historicistic" leanings by refusing to accept the apocryphal Gospels and the "unwritten sayings" as authentic documents. However, they opened the way to long controversies within the Church, and facilitated attacks on the part of non-Christians, by accepting not one Gospel but four. Since differences existed between the synoptic Gospels and the Gospel of John, they had to be explained, and justified, by exegesis.

The exegetical crisis was precipitated by Marcion, in 137. Marcion proclaimed that there was only one authentic Gospel, orally transmitted in the beginning, then written down and sedulously interpolated by enthusiastic partisans of Judaism.

Actually this "only valid" Gospel was Luke's, reduced by Marcion to what he considered the authentic kernel.[1] Marcion had used the method of the Greco-Roman grammarians, who claimed to be able to separate the mythological excrescences from antique theological texts. In defending themselves against Marcion and the other Gnostics, the orthodox were forced to employ the same method.

At the beginning of the second century Aelius Theon, in his *Progymnasmata,* showed the difference between myth and narrative: the myth is "a false account portraying truth," whereas the narrative is "an account descriptive of events which took place or might have taken place."[2] The Christian theologians, of course, denied that the Gospels were "myths" or "wonder stories." Justin, for example, could not believe that there was any danger of confusing the Gospels with "wonder stories": on the one hand, the life of Jesus was the accomplishment of the Old Testament prophecies and, on the other, the literary form of the Gospels was not that of myth. More than this: Justin held that the non-Christian reader could be given material proofs of the historical truth of the Gospels. The Nativity, for example, could be proved by the "tax declarations submitted under the procurator Quirinius and (*ex hypothesi?*) available at Rome a century later."[3] So too, a Tatian or a Clement of Alexandria considered the Gospels historical documents.

---

[1] For what follows, see Robert M. Grant, *The Earliest Lives of Jesus* (New York, 1961), pp. 10 ff.

[2] *Ibid.,* p. 15. On Theon, see *ibid.,* pp. 39 ff. Cf. also *The Letter and the Spirit* (London, 1957), pp. 120 ff., and Jean Pépin, *Mythe et Allégorie. Les origines grecques et les contestations judéo-chrétiennes* (Paris, 1958).

[3] R. M. Grant, *op. cit.,* p. 21.

But for our purpose the greatest importance attaches to
Origen. For, on the one hand, Origen was too convinced of
the spiritual value of the stories preserved by the Gospels to
admit that they could be taken in a crudely literal sense, as
simple believers and heretics took them—and for this reason
he was a partisan of allegorical exegesis. But, on the other
hand, when he was forced to defend Christianity against
Celsus, he insisted on the historicity of the life of Jesus and
attempted to substantiate all the historical testimonies. Origen
criticizes and rejects the historicity of the cleansing of the
Temple. "In Origen's systematic treatment of inspiration and
exegesis he tells us that where spiritual truths did not correspond to historical events, 'the scripture wove into the historical narrative what did not take place—at some points
what cannot take place and at others what can take place
but did not.' "[4] Instead of "myth" and "fiction," he uses
"enigma" and "parable"; but there is no doubt that for Origen
the terms are equivalent.[5]

Origen, then, admits that the Gospels contain episodes
that are not "authentic" historically though they are "true"
on the spiritual plane. But in answering Celsus' criticisms, he
also admits the difficulty of proving the historicity of a historical event. "An attempt to substantiate the truth of almost
any story as historical fact, even if the story is true, and to
produce complete certainty about it, is one of the most difficult tasks and in some cases impossible."[6]

Origen believes, however, that certain events in the life of

[4] Origen, *De principiis* 4, 2, 9, cited by Grant, *op. cit.,* p. 65.
[5] Grant, *op. cit.,* p. 66.
[6] *Contra Celsum* I, 42, cited by Grant, *op. cit.,* p. 71.

Jesus are adequately substantiated by historical testimonies. For example, Jesus was crucified in the presence of a crowd of people. The earthquake and the darkness can be confirmed by the historical narrative of Phlegon of Tralles.[7] The Last Supper is a historical event that can be dated with absolute precision.[8] So is the ordeal in Gethsemane, though the Gospel of John does not mention it (but Origen explains the reason for this silence: John is more concerned with the divinity of Jesus and he knows that God the Logos cannot be tempted). The resurrection is "true" in the historical sense of the word, because it is an event, even though the resurrected body no longer belonged to the physical world. (The resurrected body was made of air and was spiritual.)[9]

Though he does not doubt the historicity of the life, passion, and resurrection of Jesus Christ, Origen is more concerned with the spiritual, nonhistorical meaning of the Gospel text. The true meaning is "beyond history."[10] The exegetist must be able to "free himself from the historical materials," for these are only a "steppingstone." To overstress the historicity of Jesus and neglect the deeper meaning of his life and message is, in fact, to mutilate Christianity. "People marvel at Jesus," he writes in his *Commentary on the Gospel of John,* "when they look into the history about him, but they no longer believe when the deeper meaning is disclosed to them; instead, they suppose it to be false."[11]

[7] *Contra Celsum* II, 56–59, cited by Grant, *op. cit.,* p. 75.

[8] Cf. Grant, *op. cit.,* p. 93.

[9] Cf. *ibid.,* p. 78.

[10] See R. Grant, *op. cit.,* pp. 115–116, and Jean Daniélou, *Message évangélique et culture hellénistique aux IIe et IIIe siècles* (Paris, 1961), pp. 251 ff.

[11] *Commentary on John,* 20, 30, cited by Grant, *op. cit.,* p. 116.

Historical Time and liturgical Time

Origen rightly understood that the originality of Christianity lies above all in the fact that the Incarnation took place in a historical Time and not in cosmic Time. But neither does he forget that the Mystery of the Incarnation cannot be reduced to its historicity. Besides, by proclaiming the divinity of Jesus Christ "to the nations," the earliest Christian generations implicitly proclaimed his trans-historicity. This did not mean that Jesus was not a historical figure, but the emphasis was put primarily on the fact that he was the Son of God, the universal Saviour who had redeemed not only Man but Nature too. Nay, more—the historicity of Jesus had already been transcended by his Ascension to Heaven and by the fact that he had returned into the divine Glory.

In proclaiming the Incarnation, Resurrection, and Ascension of the Word, the Christians were sure that they were not putting forth a new myth. Actually, they were employing the categories of mythical thought. Obviously they could not recognize this mythical thought in the desacralized mythologies of the pagan scholars who were their contemporaries. But it is clear that for Christians of all creeds the center of religious life is constituted by the drama of Jesus Christ. Although played out in History, this drama first established the possibility of salvation; hence there is only one way to gain salvation—to reiterate this exemplary drama ritually and to imitate the supreme model revealed by the life and teaching of Jesus. Now, this type of religious behavior is integral with genuine mythical thought.

It must at once be added that, *by the very fact that it is a religion,* Christianity had to keep at least one mythical aspect

—liturgical Time, that is, the periodical recovery of the *illud tempus* of the "beginnings." "The religious experience of the Christian is based upon an *imitation* of the Christ as *exemplary pattern,* upon the liturgical repetition of the life, death, and resurrection of the Lord, and upon the *contemporaneity* of the Christian with *illud tempus* which begins with the Nativity at Bethlehem and ends, provisionally, with the Ascension." Now, as we have seen, "the imitation of a transhuman model, the repetition of an exemplary scenario and the breakaway from profane time through a moment which opens out into the Great Time, are the essential marks of 'mythical behavior' —that is, the behavior of the man of the archaic societies, who finds the very source of his existence in the myth."[12]

However, though liturgical Time is a circular Time, Christianity, as faithful heir of Judaism, accepts the linear Time of History: the World was created only once and will have only one end; the Incarnation took place only once, in historical Time, and there will be only one Judgment. From the very first, Christianity was subjected to various and conflicting influences, especially those from Gnosticism, Judaism, and "paganism." The Church's reaction was not always the same. The Fathers fought relentlessly against the acosmism and esotericism of the Gnosis; yet they kept the Gnostic elements found in the Gospel of John, in the Pauline Epistles, and in certain primitive texts. But, despite persecutions, Gnosticism was never wholly extirpated, and certain Gnostic myths, in more or less camouflaged form, reappeared in the oral and written literatures of the Middle Ages.

[12] M. Eliade, *Myths, Dreams and Mysteries,* pp. 30–31. See also Allan W. Watts, *Myth and Ritual in Christianity* (London and New York, 1953); Olivier Clément, *Transfigurer le Temps* (Neuchâtel-Paris, 1959).

As for Judaism, it gave the Church not only an allegorical method of interpreting the Scriptures, but, most importantly, the outstanding model for "historicizing" the festivals and symbols of the cosmic religion. The "Judaization" of primitive Christianity is equivalent to its "historicization," that is, to the decision of the first theologians to connect the history of Jesus' preaching and of the earliest Church to the Sacred History of the people of Israel. But Judaism had "historicized" a certain number of seasonal festivals and cosmic symbols by connecting them with important events in the history of Israel (cf. the Feast of Tabernacles, Passover, the Hanukkah Feast of Lights, etc.). The Church Fathers took the same course: they "Christianized" Asianic and Mediterranean rites and myths by connecting them with a "Sacred History." Obviously, this "Sacred History" exceeded the bounds of the Old Testament and now included the New Testament, the preaching of the Apostles, and, later, the history of the Saints. A certain number of cosmic symbols—Water, the Tree and the Vine, the plow and the ax, the ship, the chariot, etc.— had already been assimilated by Judaism,[13] and they could easily be incorporated into the doctrine and practice of the Church by being given a sacramental or ecclesiological meaning.

"Cosmic Christianity"

The real difficulties arose later, when the Christian missionaries were faced, especially in Central and Western Europe,

---

[13] Cf. Erwin Goodenough, *Jewish Symbols in the Greco-Roman Period,* vols. VII–VIII: *Pagan Symbols in Judaism* (New York, 1958); Jean Daniélou, *Les symboles chrétiens primitifs* (Paris, 1961).

by *living* popular religions. Willy-nilly, they ended by "Christianizing" the "pagan" divine Figures and myths that resisted extirpation. A large number of dragon-slaying Gods or Heroes became St. Georges; storm Gods were transformed into St. Eliases; the countless fertility Goddesses were assimilated to the Virgin or to female Saints. It could even be said that a part of the popular religion of pre-Christian Europe survived, either camouflaged or transformed, in the feasts of the Church calendar and in the cult of the Saints. For more than ten centuries the Church was obliged to fight the continual influx of "pagan" elements—that is, elements belonging to the cosmic religion—into Christian practices and legends. The success of this intensive struggle was not very great, especially in the South and Southeast of Europe. In the folklore and religious practices of the rural populations at the end of the nineteenth century there still survived figures, myths, and rituals from earliest antiquity, or even from protohistory.[14]

The Orthodox and Roman Catholic Churches have been criticized for accepting so many pagan elements. It is a question if these criticisms were always justified. On the one hand, "paganism" could survive only in "Christianized" form, even if at times the Christianization was rather superficial. This policy of assimilating the "paganism" that could not be destroyed was nothing new; the primitive Church had already accepted and assimilated a large part of the pre-Christian sacred calendar. On the other hand, the peasants, because of their own mode of existing in the Cosmos, were not attracted

---

[14] Leopold Schmidt has shown that the agricultural folklore of Central Europe contains mythological and ritual elements that had vanished from classic Greek mythology even before the times of Homer and Hesiod; cf. L. Schmidt, *Gestaltheiligkeit im bäuerlichen Arbeitsmythos* (Vienna, 1952), especially pp. 136 ff.

by a "historical" and moral Christianity. The religious experience peculiar to the rural populations was nourished by what could be called a "cosmic Christianity." In other words, the peasants of Europe understood Christianity as a cosmic liturgy. The Christological mystery also involved the destiny of the Cosmos. "All Nature sighs, awaiting the Resurrection" is a central motif not only in the Easter liturgy but also in the religious folklore of Eastern Christianity. Mystical empathy with the cosmic rhythms, which was violently attacked by the Old Testament prophets and barely tolerated by the Church, is central to the religions of rural populations, especially in Southeastern Europe. For this whole section of Christendom "Nature" is not the World of sin but the work of God. After the Incarnation, the World had been re-established in its original glory; this is why Christ and the Church had been imbued with so many cosmic symbols. In the religious folklore of Southeastern Europe the sacraments sanctify Nature too.

For the peasants of Eastern Europe this in no sense implied a "paganization" of Christianity, but, on the contrary, a "Christianization" of the religion of their ancestors. When the time comes for the history of this "popular theology" to be written on the evidence that can be traced in seasonal festivals and religious folklores, it will be realized that "cosmic Christianity" is not a new form of paganism or a pagan-Christian syncretism. Rather it is an original religious creation, in which eschatology and soteriology are given cosmic dimensions. Even more significantly, Christ, while remaining the Pantocrator, comes down to Earth and visits the peasants, just as, in the myths of archaic peoples, the Supreme Being was wont to do before he became a *deus otiosus;* this Christ is not "historical," since popular thought is interested neither in chronology nor in the accuracy of events and the authenticity of historical figures. This does not mean that, for the rural populations, Christ is only a "God" inherited from the old polytheisms. For, on the one hand, there is no contradiction between the Christ image of the Gospels and the Church and the Christ image of religious folklore. The Nativity, the teaching of Jesus, and his miracles, the Crucifixion and the Resurrection are essential themes in this popular Christianity. On the other hand, it is a *Christian spirit*—not a pagan spirit —that impregnates all these folklore creations; they tell of man's salvation by Christ; of faith, hope, and charity; of a World that is "good" because it was created by God the Father and redeemed by the Son; of a human existence that will not be repeated and that is not without meaning; man is free to choose good or evil, but he will not be judged solely by that choice.

It does not lie within the scope of this book to outline this "popular theology." But it is obvious that the cosmic Christianity of the rural populations is dominated by nostalgia for a Nature sanctified by the presence of Jesus. It is, in some sort, a nostalgia for Paradise, the desire to find again a trans- figured and invulnerable Nature, safe from the cataclysms brought by wars, devastation, and conquests. It is also the expression of the "ideal" of these agricultural societies, constantly terrorized by allogeneous warrior hordes and exploited by the various classes of more or less autochthonous "masters." It is a passive revolt against the tragedy and injustice of History, in the last analysis against the fact that evil proves to be no longer only an individual decision but, increasingly, a transpersonal structure of the historical World.

But to return to our theme, it is clear that this popular Christianity has kept alive certain categories of mythical thought even down to our day.

Eschatological mythologies of the Middle Ages

In the Middle Ages we witness an upwelling of mythical thought. All the social classes depend on their mythological traditions. Knights, artisans, clerks, peasants, accept an "origin myth" for their condition and endeavor to imitate an exemplary model. These mythologies have various sources. The Arthurian cycle and the Grail theme incorporate, under a varnish of Christianity, a number of Celtic beliefs, especially those having to do with the Other World. The knights try to follow the example of Lancelot or Parsifal. The trouvères elaborate a whole mythology of woman and Love, making use of Christian elements but going beyond or contradicting Church doctrine.

It is especially in certain historical movements of the Middle Ages that we find the most typical manifestations of mythical thought. Millennialist exaltation and eschatological myths come to the fore in the Crusades, in the movements of a Tanchelm and an Eudes de l'Etoile, in the elevation of Frederick II to the rank of Messiah, and in many other collective messianic, utopian, and prerevolutionary phenomena, which have been brilliantly treated by Norman Cohn in his *The Pursuit of the Millennium.* To dwell for a moment on the mythological aureole of Frederick II: the imperial chancellor, Pietro della Vigna, presents his master as a cosmic Saviour; the whole World was awaiting such a Cosmocrator, and now the flames of evil are extinguished, swords are beaten into plowshares, peace, justice and security are firmly installed. "More than all this—Frederick possesses a unique virtue which binds the elements of the universe together, reconciling heat with cold, the solid with the liquid, all opposites with one another. He is a cosmic messiah whom land and sea and air unite in adoring. And his coming is a work of divine providence; for the world was sinking toward its end, the Last Judgment was already at hand, when God in his great mercy granted a reprieve and sent this pure ruler to make an age of peace and order and harmony in the Last Days. That these phrases fairly reflected Frederick's own view is shown by the letter which he addressed to his birthplace, Jesi near Ancona; for there he makes it quite clear that he regards his own birth as an event possessing the same significance for mankind as the birth of Christ and Jesi as a second Bethlehem. Probably alone among medieval monarchs, Frederick believed himself to be divine in virtue not of his office but of his inborn nature—nothing less than incarnate God."[15]

The mythology of Frederick II did not disappear with his death, for the simple reason that his death could not be believed: the Emperor must have retired to a distant country, or, according to the most popular legend, he was sleeping under Mount Aetna. But one day he would wake again and return to claim his throne. And in fact, thirty-four years after his death an impostor was able to convince the city of Neuss that he was Frederick II *redivivus*. Even after this pseudo-Frederick was executed at Wetzlar, the myth did not lose its virulence. In the fifteenth century it was still believed that

[15] Norman Cohn, *The Pursuit of the Millennium*, p. 104. On the messianic claims of Frederick II, cf. E. Kantorowitz, *Frederick the Second, 1194–1250* (English trans., London, 1931), pp. 450 ff., 511 ff.; N. Cohn, pp. 103 ff.

Frederick was alive and would live until the end of the World, in short, that he was the only legitimate Emperor and that there would never be another.

The myth of Frederick II is only a famous example of a far more widespread and persistent phenomenon. In fact, the religious prestige and eschatological function of kings survived in Europe to the seventeenth century. The secularization of the concept of eschatological King did not extinguish the hope, deeply rooted in the collective soul, for a universal renewal brought about by the exemplary Hero in one of his new forms—the Reformer, the Revolutionary, the Martyr (in the name of the freedom of peoples), the Party Leader. The role and mission of the Founders and Leaders of the modern totalitarian movements include a considerable number of eschatological and soteriological elements. Mythical thought transcends and discards some of its earlier expressions, outmoded by History, and adapts itself to the new social conditions and new cultural fashions—but it resists extirpation.

As to the Crusade phenomenon, Alphonse Dupront has well demonstrated its mythical structures and eschatological orientation. "At the center of a Crusade consciousness, in the cleric as in the non-cleric, is the duty to free Jerusalem. . . . What is most strongly expressed in the Crusade is a twofold fulfillment: an accomplishment of the times and an accomplishment of human space. In the sense, for space, that the sign of the accomplishment of the times is the gathering of the nations about the sacred mother city, the center of the world, Jerusalem."[16]

[16] Alphonse Dupront, "Croisades et eschatologie," in *Umanesimo e esoterismo*. Atti del V Convegno Internazionale di Studi Umanistici, a cura di Enrico Castelli (Padua, 1960), p. 177.

The proof that we are here in the presence of a collective spiritual phenomenon, of an irrational drive, is, among other things, the Children's Crusades that suddenly began in Northern France and Germany in the year 1212. The spontaneity of these movements appears to be beyond doubt: "No one urging them, either from foreign lands or from their own," says a contemporary witness.[17] Children "having at once two characteristics that were signs of the extraordinary, their extreme youth and their poverty, especially little herd-boys,"[18] took the road, and the poor joined them. There were perhaps thirty thousand of them, and they walked in procession, singing. When asked where they were going, they answered: "To God." According to a contemporary chronicler, "their intention was to cross the sea and do what kings and the mighty had not done, to recapture Christ's Sepulchre."[19] The clergy had opposed this rising of children. The French crusade ended in catastrophe. Reaching Marseilles, they embarked in seven large ships, but two of these ran aground in a storm off Sardinia and all the passengers were drowned. As for the other five ships, the two treacherous shipowners took them to Alexandria, where they sold the children to the Saracen leaders and to slave dealers.

The "German" crusade followed the same pattern. A contemporary chronicle tells that in 1212 "there appeared a boy named Nicolas who gathered around him a multitude of children and women. He affirmed that, by order of an angel, he must go with them to Jerusalem to free the Saviour's cross and that the sea, as formerly for the people of Israel, would let

---

[17] Paul Alphandéry and Alphonse Dupront, *La Chrétienté et l'idée de Croisade* (Paris, 1959), vol. II, p. 118.

[18] *Ibid.*, p. 119.

[19] Reinier, cited by P. Alphandéry and A. Dupront, *op. cit.*, p. 120.

them pass dryshod."[20] They were unarmed. Starting from the region around Cologne, they traveled down the Rhine, crossed the Alps, and reached Northern Italy. Some of them got as far as Genoa and Pisa, but they were turned back. Those who managed to reach Rome were obliged to admit that they were backed by no authority. The Pope disapproved of their project, and they were forced to return. As the chronicler of the *Annales Marbacenses* puts it, "they came back starving and barefoot, one by one and in silence." No one helped them. Another witness writes: "The greater part of them lay dead from hunger in villages, in public places, and no one buried them."[21]

P. Alphandéry and A. Dupront have rightly recognized in these movements the elect role of the child in popular piety. It is at once the myth of the Holy Innocents, the exaltation of the child by Jesus, and the popular reaction against the Crusade of the Barons, the same reaction that appeared in the legends that crystallized around the "Tafurs" of the earliest Crusades.[22] "The reconquest of the Holy Places can no longer be expected except from a miracle—and the miracle can only come about in favor of the purest, of children and the poor."[23]

Survivals of the eschatological myth

The failure of the Crusades did not put an end to eschatological hopes. In his *De Monarchia Hispanica* (1600), To-

---

[20] *Annales Scheftlariensis,* text cited by Alphandéry-Dupront, *op. cit.,* p. 123.

[21] Texts cited by Alphandéry-Dupront, *op. cit.,* p. 127.

[22] On the "Tafurs," cf. also Norman Cohn, *The Pursuit of the Millennium,* pp. 45 ff.

[23] P. Alphandéry and A. Dupront, *op. cit.,* p. 145.

masso Campanella begged the King of Spain to furnish the money for a new Crusade against the Turkish Empire, and, after the victory, to establish the Universal Monarchy. Thirty-eight years later, in the *Ecloga* addressed to Louis XIII and Anne of Austria to celebrate the birth of the future Louis XIV, Campanella prophesies the *recuperatio Terrae Sanctae,* and, with it, the *renovatio saeculi.* The young king will conquer the whole Earth in a thousand days, laying the monsters low, that is, subduing the kingdoms of the infidels and freeing Greece. Mohammed will be driven out of Europe; Egypt and Ethiopia will again be Christian, the Tartars, the Persians, the Chinese and the whole East will be converted. All peoples will be united in one Christendom and this regenerated Universe will have one Center—Jerusalem. "The Church," Campanella writes, "began at Jerusalem, and to Jerusalem it will return, after circling the world."[24] In his treatise *La prima e la seconda resurrezione,* Campanella no longer sees the conquest of Jerusalem, in the manner of St. Bernard, as a stage on the way to the Celestial Jerusalem but as the establishment of the messianic reign.[25]

It is needless to multiply examples. But it is important to stress the continuity between the medieval eschatological conceptions and the various "philosophies of History" produced by the Enlightenment and the nineteenth century. During the last thirty years it has begun to be realized what an exceptional role was played by the "prophecies" of Gioacchino da Fiore in instigating and articulating all these messianic movements that arose in the thirteenth century and continued,

[24] Campanella's note to verse 207 of his *Ecloga,* cited by A. Dupront, "Croisades et eschatologie," p. 187.

[25] Critical edition by Romano Amerio (Rome, 1955), p. 72; A. Dupront, *op. cit.,* 189.

in more or less secularized form, into the nineteenth.[26] Gioacchino's central idea—that is, the imminent entrance of the
World into the third age of History, which will be the age of
freedom since it will be realized under the sign of the Holy
Spirit—had considerable repercussions. This idea ran counter
to the theology of History accepted by the Church from the
time of St. Augustine. According to the current doctrine, perfection having been achieved on Earth by the Church, there
will be no *renovatio* in the future. The only decisive event will
be the Second Coming of Christ and the Last Judgment. Gioacchino da Fiore brings back into Christianity the archaic myth
of universal regeneration. To be sure, it is no longer a periodic
and indefinitely repeatable regeneration. Yet it is none the less
true that Gioacchino conceives the third age as the reign of
Freedom, under the guidance of the Holy Spirit—which
implies transcending historical Christianity and, in the last
analysis, abolishing all existing rules and institutions.

We cannot here present the various eschatological movements inspired by Gioacchino. But we must at least refer to
some unexpected continuations of the Calabrian· prophet's
ideas. Thus, for example, Lessing in his *Education of the
Human Race* elaborates the thesis of continual and progressive revelation culminating in a third age. To be sure, Les-

[26] Ernesto Bonaiuti deserves the greatest credit for having begun the
revival of Gioacchinian studies with his edition of the *Tractatus super
quatuor Evangelia* (Rome, 1930) and his book *Gioacchino da Fiore*
(Rome, 1931). Cf. also his two important articles: "Prolegomeni alla
storia di Gioacchino da Fiore" (*Ricerche Religiose,* vol. IV [1928]) and
"Il misticismo di Gioacchino da Fiore" (*ibid.,* vol. V [1929]), reprinted
in the posthumous volume *Saggi di Storia del Cristianesimo* (Vicenza,
1957), pp. 327–382. See also Ernst Benz, "Die Kategorien der religiösen
Geschichtsdeutung Joachims" (*Zeitschrift für Kirchengeschichte* [1931],
pp. 24–111) and *Ecclesia Spiritualis* (Stuttgart, 1934).

sing thought of this third age as the triumph of reason through education; but it was none the less, he believed, the fulfill-ment of Christian revelation, and he refers with sympathy and admiration to "certain enthusiasts of the thirteenth and fourteenth centuries," whose only error lay in proclaiming the "new eternal Gospel" too soon.[27] Lessing's ideas aroused some repercussions and, through the disciples of Saint-Simon, he probably influenced Auguste Comte and his doctrine of the three stages. Fichte, Hegel, Schelling were influenced, though for different reasons, by the Gioacchinian myth of an imminent third age that will renew and complete History. Through them this eschatological myth influenced certain Russian writers, especially Krasinsky, with his *Third Kingdom of the Spirit,* and Merejkowsky, author of *The Christianity of the Third Testament.*[28] To be sure, we are now dealing with semiphilosophical ideologies and fantasies and no longer with the eschatological expectation of the reign of the Holy Spirit. But the myth of universal renovation in a more or less imminent future is still discernible in all these theories and fantasies.

"The myths of the modern world"

Some forms of "mythical behavior" still survive in our day. This does not mean that they represent "survivals" of an archaic mentality. But certain aspects and functions of myth-

[27] Cf. Karl Löwith, *Meaning in History* (Chicago, 1949), p. 208.

[28] Karl Löwith, *ibid.,* p. 210, draws attention to the fact that this last work inspired *Das dritte Reich* by the Russo-German author H. Moeller van der Bruck. Cf. also Jakob Taubes, *Abendländische Eschatologien* (Bern, 1947), who compares Hegel's philosophy of history with Gioac-chino da Fiore's.

ical thought are constituents of the human being. We have discussed some "myths of the modern world" elsewhere.[29] The problem is complex and absorbing; we cannot hope to exhaust in a few pages what would furnish the material for a large volume. We will confine ourselves to briefly discussing some aspects of "modern mythologies."

We have seen the importance of the "return to the origins" in archaic societies, a return that can be effected in a number of ways. Now, this prestige of the "origin" has also survived in the societies of Europe. When an innovation was to be made, it was conceived, or presented, as a return to the origin. The Reformation began the return to the Bible and dreamed of recovering the experience of the primitive Church, or even of the earliest Christian communities. The French Revolution had its paradigmatic models in the Romans and the Spartans. The inspirers and leaders of the first successful radical revolution in Europe, which marked not merely the end of a regime but the end of a historical cycle, thought of themselves as restoring the ancient virtues praised by Livy and Plutarch.

At the dawn of the modern World the "origin" enjoyed an almost magical prestige. To have a well-established "origin" meant, when all was said and done, to have the advantage of a noble origin. "We find our origin in Rome!" the Romanian intellectuals of the eighteenth and nineteenth centuries proudly repeated. In their case consciousness of Latin descent was accompanied by a kind of mystical participation in the greatness of Rome. Similarly the Hungarian intelligentsia found a justification for the antiquity, nobility, and historical mission of the Magyars in the origin myth of Hunor and Magor and in the heroic saga of Arpad. All

[29] Cf. Eliade, *Myths, Dreams and Mysteries*, pp. 23–38.

through Central and Southeastern Europe at the beginning of the nineteenth century the mirage of "noble origin" aroused nothing short of a passion for national history, especially for its earliest phases. "A people without history" (read: without "historical documents" or without historiography) "is as if it did not exist!" This anxiety is perceptible in all the national historians of Central and Eastern Europe. Such a passion for national historiography was, to be sure, a consequence of the awakening of nationalities in this part of Europe. Then too, it was soon transformed into an instrument of propaganda and political warfare. But the desire to prove the "noble origin" and "antiquity" of one's people dominates Southeastern Europe to such an extent that, with few exceptions, all of the respective historians confined themselves to national history and finally wound up in cultural provincialism.

The passion for "noble origin" also explains the racist myth of "Aryanism" which periodically gains currency in the West, especially in Germany. The socio-political contexts of this myth are too well known to require discussion. What is of concern for our study is the fact that the "Aryan" represented at once the "primordial" Ancestor and the noble "hero," the latter laden with all the virtues that still haunted those who had not managed to reconcile themselves to the ideal of the societies that emerged from the revolutions of 1789 and 1848. The "Aryan" was the exemplary model that must be imitated in order to recover racial "purity," physical strength, nobility, the heroic "ethics" of the glorious and creative "beginnings."

As for Marxist Communism, its eschatological and millennialist structures have been duly noted. We remarked not long ago that Marx had taken over one of the great eschatological myths of the Asianico-Mediterranean world: the redeeming role of the Just Man (in our day, the proletariat), whose sufferings are destined to change the ontological status of the World. "In fact, Marx's classless society, and the consequent disappearance of all historical tensions, find their most exact precedent in the myth of the Golden Age which, according to a number of traditions, lies at the beginning and the end of History. Marx has enriched this venerable myth with a truly messianic Judaeo-Christian idealogy; on the one hand, by the prophetic and soteriological function he ascribes to the proletariat; and, on the other, by the final struggle between Good and Evil, which may well be compared with the apocalyptic conflict between Christ and Antichrist, ending in the decisive victory of the former. It is indeed significant that Marx turns to his own account the Judaeo-Christian eschatological hope of an *absolute* [*end to*] *History;* in that he parts company from the other historical philosophers (Croce, for instance, and Ortega y Gasset), for whom the tensions of history are implicit in the human condition, and therefore can never be completely abolished."[30]

Myths and mass media

Recent studies have brought out the mythical structures of the images and behavior patterns imposed on collectivities by mass media. This phenomenon is found especially in the United States.[31] The characters of the comic strips present

[30] *Ibid.,* pp. 25–26.
[31] Cf., for example, Coulton Waugh, *The Comics* (New York, 1947); Stephen Becker, *Comic Art in America* (New York, 1960); Umberto Eco, "Il Mito di Superman," in: *Demitizzazione e Imagine,* a cura di Enrico Castelli (Padua, 1962), pp. 131–148.

the modern version of mythological or folklore Heroes. They incarnate the ideal of a large part of society, to such a degree that any change in their typical conduct or, still worse, their death, will bring on veritable crises among their readers; the latter react violently, and protest by sending thousands of telegrams to the authors of the comic strips or the editors of the newspapers in which they appear. A fantastic character, Superman, has become extremely popular, especially because of his double identity; although coming from a planet destroyed by a catastrophe, and possessing prodigious powers, Superman lives on Earth in the modest guise of a journalist, Clark Kent; he is timid, unassertive, dominated by his colleague Lois Lane. This humiliating camouflage of a Hero whose powers are literally unlimited revives a well-known mythical theme. In the last analysis, the myth of Superman satisfies the secret longings of modern man who, though he knows that he is a fallen, limited creature, dreams of one day proving himself an "exceptional person," a "Hero."

Much the same could be said of the detective novel. On the one hand, the reader witnesses the exemplary struggle between Good and Evil, between the Hero (= the Detective) and the criminal (the modern incarnation of the Demon). On the other, through an unconscious process of projection and identification, he takes part in the mystery and the drama and has the feeling that he is personally involved in a paradigmatic —that is, a dangerous, "heroic"—action.

The mythicization of public figures through the mass media, the transformation of a personality into an exemplary image, has also been analyzed. "Lloyd Warner tells us of the creation of such a public figure in the first section of his *The*

Living and the Dead. Biggy Muldoon, a Yankee City politican who became a national figure because of his colorful opposition to the Hill Street Aristocracy, had a demagogic public image built up by the press and radio. He was presented as a crusading man of the people attacking intrenched wealth. Then, when the public tired of this image, the mass media obligingly turned Biggy into a villain, a corrupt politician seeking personal profit out of the public necessity. Warner points out that the real Biggy was considerably different from either image but actually was forced to modify his style of action to conform to one image and fight the other."[32]

Mythical behavior can be recognized in the obsession with "success" that is so characteristic of modern society and that expresses an obscure wish to transcend the limits of the human condition; in the exodus to Suburbia, in which we can detect the nostalgia for "primordial perfection"; in the paraphernalia and emotional intensity that characterize what has been called the "cult of the sacred automobile." As Andrew Greeley remarks, "one need merely visit the annual automobile show to realize that it is a highly ritualized religious performance. The colors, the lights, the music, the awe of the worshippers, the presence of the temple priestesses (fashion models), the pomp and splendor, the lavish waste of money, the thronging crowds—all these would represent in any other culture a clearly liturgical service. . . . The cult of the sacred car has its adepts and initiati. No gnostic more eagerly awaited a revelation from an oracle than does an automobile worshipper await the first rumors about the new models. It is at this time

[32] Andrew Greeley, "Myths, Symbols and Rituals in the Modern World," *The Critic,* vol. XX, no. 3 (December, 1961, January, 1962), p. 19.

of the annual seasonal cycle that the high priests of the cult—the auto dealers—take on a new importance as an anxious public eagerly expects the coming of a new form of salvation."[33]

Myths of the elite

Less attention has been paid to what could be called the myths of the elite, especially those crystallized around artistic creation and its cultural and social repercussions. These myths, be it said, have succeeded in imposing themselves far beyond the closed corporation of the initiate, principally because of the inferiority complex that now afflicts both the public and official art circles. The aggressive incomprehension of the public, of critics, and of the official representatives of art toward a Rimbaud or a Van Gogh, the disastrous consequences —especially for collectors and museums—produced by indifference toward innovating movements, from impressionism to cubism and surrealism, have been hard lessons for the critics and the public as well as for art dealers, museum directors, and collectors. Today their only fear is not to be advanced enough and hence not to be in time to recognize genius in a work that is at first sight unintelligible. Perhaps never before in history has the artist been so certain that the more daring, iconoclastic, absurd, and inaccessible he is, the more he will be recognized, praised, spoiled, idolatrized. In some countries the result has even been an academicism in reverse, the academicism of the "avant-garde"—to such a point that any artistic experience that makes no concessions to this new conformism is in danger of being stifled or ignored.

The myth of the damned artist, which obsessed the nine-

[33] *Ibid.*, p. 24.

teenth century, is outmoded today. Especially in the United States, but also in Western Europe, audacity and defiance have long since ceased to be harmful to an artist. On the contrary, he is asked to conform to his mythical image, that is, to be strange, irreducible, and to "produce something new." It is the absolute triumph of the permanent revolution in art. "Anything goes" is no longer an adequate formulation: now every novelty is considered a stroke of genius beforehand and put on the same plane as the innovations of a Van Gogh or a Picasso, even if the artist only mutilates a poster or signs a sardine tin.

The significance of this cultural phenomenon is the greater because, perhaps for the first time in the history of art, there is no longer any tension between artists, critics, collectors, and the public. They are all in agreement always, and long before a new work is created or an unknown artist discovered. The one thing that matters is not to have to say later that one did not understand the importance of a new artistic experience.

We cannot, of course, here analyze the mythology of the modern elites in all its manifestations. We shall confine ourselves to a few remarks. First of all, we may note the redeeming function of "difficulty," especially as found in works of modern art. If the elite revel in *Finnegans Wake,* or in atonal music, or in *tachisme,* it is also because such works represent closed worlds, hermetic universes that cannot be entered except by overcoming immense difficulties, like the initiatory ordeals of the archaic and traditional societies. On the one hand, one has the experience of an "initiation," an experience that has almost vanished from the modern World; on the other hand, one proclaims to the "others" (i.e., the "mass") that one belongs to a select minority—not, as once, to an aristocracy (for modern elites lean toward the left), but to a gnosis that has the advantage of being at once spiritual and secular in that it opposes both official values and the traditional churches. Through their cult of extravagant originality, of difficulty, of incomprehensibility, the elites advertise their escape from the banal universe of their parents while at the same time revolting against certain contemporary philosophies of despair.

Basically, being fascinated by the difficulty, not to say the incomprehensibility, of works of art expresses the desire to discover a new, secret, hitherto unknown meaning for the World and human life. One dreams of being "initiated" and thereby made able to understand the occult meaning of all these destructions of artistic languages, these "original" experiences that, at first sight, no longer seem to have anything in common with art. The torn posters, the empty, scorched, slashed canvases, the "art objects" that explode on opening day, the improvised plays in which the actors' speeches are drawn by lot—*all this must have a meaning,* just as certain incomprehensible words in *Finnegans Wake* come to be fraught with many meanings and values and with a strange beauty for the initiate when he discovers that they are derived from modern Greek or Swahili words disfigured by aberrant consonants, and enriched by secret allusions to possible puns when they are spoken aloud and very fast.

To be sure, all the genuine revolutionary experiences of modern art reflect certain aspects of the contemporary spiritual crisis or at least of the crisis in artistic knowledge and creation. But what concerns our investigation is the fact that the "elites" find in the extravagance and unintelligibility of modern works the opportunity for an initiatory gnosis. It is a "new World" being built up from ruins and enigmas, an almost private World, which one would like to keep for oneself and a very few initiates. But the prestige of difficulty and incomprehensibility is such that, very soon, the "public" too is conquered and proclaims its total acceptance of the elite's discoveries.

The destruction of artistic languages was accomplished by cubism, dadaism, and surrealism, by atonality and "musique concrète," by James Joyce, Becket, and Ionesco. Only the epigones are left furiously demolishing what has already been demolished. For, as we pointed out in an earlier chapter, the genuine creators are not willing to take their stand on ruins. Everything leads us to believe that the reduction of "artistic Universes" to the primordial state of *materia prima* is only a phase in a more complex process; just as in the cyclic conceptions of the archaic and traditional societies "Chaos," the regression of all forms to the indistinction of the *materia prima*, is followed by a new Creation, which can be homologized with a cosmogony.

We cannot here develop and refine these few observations, for the crisis in the modern arts is only of subsidiary concern to our study. Yet we must dwell for a moment on the situation and the role of literature, especially of epic literature, for it is not unrelated to mythology and mythical behavior. We do not intend to discuss the "origins" of epic literature; it is well known that, like the other literary genres, the epic and the novel continue mythological narrative, though on a different plane and in pursuit of different ends. In both cases it is a question of telling a significant story, of relating a series of dramatic events that took place in a more or less fabulous past. There is no need to go over the long and complex process that transformed some particular "mythological material" into the "subject" of an epic. What we consider important is the fact that in modern societies the prose narrative, especially the novel, has taken the place of the recitation of myths in traditional and popular societies. More than this—it is possible to dissect out the "mythical" structure of certain modern novels, in other words, to show the literary survival of great mythological themes and characters. (This is true especially in regard to the initiatory theme, the theme of the ordeals of the Hero-Redeemer and his battles with monsters, the mythologies of Woman and of Wealth.) From this point of view we could say, then, that the modern passion for the novel expresses the desire to hear the greatest possible number of "mythological stories" desacralized or simply camouflaged under "profane" forms.

No less significant is the fact that people feel the need to read "histories" and narratives that could be called paradigmatic, since they proceed in accordance with a traditional model. Whatever the gravity of the present crisis of the novel, it is none the less true that the need to find one's way into "foreign" Universes and to follow the complications of a "story" seems to be consubstantial with the human condition and hence irreducible. It is a difficult need to define, being at once desire to communicate with "others," with "strangers," and share in their dramas and hopes, and at the same time the need to know what *can have taken place*. It is hard to conceive of a human being who is not fascinated by "narrative," that is, by a recounting of significant events, by what has happened to men endowed with the "twofold reality" of literary characters (for, on the one hand, they reflect the historical and psychological reality of members of a modern society and, on the other, they possess all the magical power of an imaginary creation).

But it is especially the "escape from Time" brought about by reading—most effectively by novel reading—that connects the function of literature with that of mythologies. To be sure, the time that one "lives" when reading a novel is not the time that a member of a traditional society recovers when he listens to a myth. But in both cases alike, one "escapes" from historical and personal time and is submerged in a time that is fabulous and trans-historical. The reader is confronted with a strange, imaginary time, whose rhythms vary indefinitely, for each narrative has its own time that is peculiar to it and to it alone. The novel does not have access to the primordial time of myths, but in so far as he tells a credible story, the novelist employs a time that is *seemingly historical* yet is condensed or prolonged, a time, then, that has at its command all the freedoms of imaginary worlds.

More strongly than any of the other arts, we feel in literature a revolt against historical time, the desire to attain to other temporal rhythms than that in which we are condemned to live and work. One wonders whether the day will come when this desire to transcend one's own time—personal, historical time—and be submerged in a "strange" time, whether ecstatic or imaginary, will be completely rooted out. As long as it persists, we can say that modern man preserves at least some residues of "mythological behavior." Traces of such a mythological behavior can also be deciphered in the desire to rediscover the intensity with which one experienced or knew something *for the first time;* and also in the desire to recover the distant past, the blissful period of the "beginnings."

Here too, as we might expect, there is always the struggle against Time, the hope to be freed from the weight of "dead Time," of the Time that crushes and kills.

Appendix I.

Myths and Fairy Tales*

JAN DE VRIES has recently published a short book on fairy tales (Jan de Vries, *Betrachtungen zum Märchen, besonders in seinem Verhältnis zu Heldensage und Mythos,* Helsinki, 1954). As the title indicates, his considerations have to do chiefly with the relations of folk tales to heroic saga and myth. This is a vast and formidable subject, with which no one was more qualified to cope than the eminent Dutch Germanist and folklorist. His little book lays no claim to exhausting all the aspects of the problem in 180 pages. It is in no sense a manual. The author set out to take provisional stock of a century of research, and especially to record the new perspectives lately opened to the specialist in folk tales. There has, of course, been a recent revival of activity in their interpretation. On the one hand, folklorists have profited by the progress achieved by ethnology, the history of religions, and depth psychology; on the other, the specialists in folk tales have themselves made a marked effort to subject their researches to a stricter methodology—witness the penetrating studies by an André Jolles or a Max Lüthi.

Jan de Vries has undertaken to present this entire movement before expounding his own views on the relations among myth, saga, and folk tale. The discussion naturally opens with an examination of the "Finnish School." Its merits are too well known to require comment. The Scandinavian scholars have done exact and extensive work: they have recorded and classified all the variants of a tale and have tried to trace their routes of dissemination. But these formal and statistical studies have solved

* *La Nouvelle Revue Française,* May, 1956.

none of the essential problems. The Finnish School has held that by meticulous study of the variants they could arrive at the "primordial form" (*Urform*) of a tale. Unfortunately, this was an illusion: in most cases the *Urform* was only one of the many pre-forms that have come down to us. This famous "primordial form"—which obsessed a whole generation of investigators—had only a hypothetical existence (J. de Vries, p. 20).

The author then discusses the French folklorist Paul Saintyves and his ritualistic theory. Saintyves's chief book, *Les Contes de Perrault et les récits parallèles* (1923) can still be read with interest and profit despite the gaps in his information and his methodological confusions. It must be admitted that his choice was not a happy one. Perrault's tales do not always constitute proper material for a comparative study. "Puss in Boots," for example, is documented neither in Scandinavia nor in Germany; in the latter country it only appears quite late and under Perrault's influence. Nevertheless, Saintyves deserves credit for recognizing in the tales ritual motifs that still survive in the religious institutions of primitive peoples. On the other hand, he was simply wrong in supposing that he had found in the tales the "text" that accompanied the rite (de Vries, p. 30). In a book that unfortunately escaped de Vries's attention, *Istoritcheskie korni volshenboi skazki* (Leningrad, 1946), the Soviet folklorist V. I. Propp returned to and developed Saintyves's ritualistic hypothesis. Propp sees in folk tales the memory of totemic initiation rites. The initiatory structure of folk tales is obvious, and will be considered later. But the whole problem is to determine whether the tale describes a system of rites belonging to a particular stage of culture, or if its initiatory scenario is "imaginary," in the sense that it is not bound up with a historico-cultural context but instead expresses an ahistorical, archetypal behavior pattern of the psyche. To give only one example: Propp refers to totemic initiations; this type of initiation was strictly closed to women; but the chief character in Slavic tales is precisely a woman—the Old Witch, the Baba Jaga. In other words, we never find in folk tales an accurate memory of a particular stage of culture; cultural styles and historical cycles are telescoped in them. All that remains is the structure of an exemplary behavior—that is, one that can be vitally experienced in a great number of cultural cycles and at many historical moments.

W. E. Peuckert's hypothesis, brilliantly discussed by Jan de Vries (pp. 30 f.), runs into similar difficulties. According to this scholar, folk tales originated in the eastern Mediterranean during the Neolithic period; and they still preserve the structure of a socio-cultural complex that includes the matriarchy, initiation, and marriage rites typical of agriculturalists. Peuckert cites the ordeals imposed on the hero of a certain type of folk tale before he can marry the daughter of the demon, and compares them with the matrimonial customs in force among agriculturalists— to gain his wife, the suitor must reap a field, build a house, etc. But, as Jan de Vries remarks, ordeals prescribed for marriage are also documented in the epic (e.g., the *Rāmāyana*) and the heroic saga. Now, it is difficult to find a place for the saga, which is essentially aristocratic poetry, in the cultural horizon of cultivators. Hence the supposed genetic relation: "matrimonial ordeals of peasant type"—"folk tale" does not necessarily hold. Elsewhere Peuckert seeks the "origin" of folk tales in the protohistorical Near East, arguing from its extraordinary economic wealth and the unprecedented flowering of fertility cults and sexual symbolism there; but Max Lüthi's analyses have shown that the erotic plays no role whatever in folk tales.

Jan de Vries devotes a lengthy discussion to C. W. von Sydow's hypothesis of the Indo-European origin of folk tales (pp. 48 f., 60 f.). The difficulties of this hypothesis are so obvious that they make it unnecessary to dwell on it, and von Sydow himself has been led to change his views. He now inclines to put the "birth" of folk tales even farther back in the past, and specifically in the Pre-Indo-European Megalithic culture. In a recent study, "Märchen und Megalithreligion" (*Paideuma*, V, 1950), Otto Huth has adopted this point of view, and it is regrettable that Jan de Vries did not consider it necessary to examine it. According to Otto Huth, the two dominant motifs of folk tales, the journey to the beyond and wedding ceremonies of royal type, belong to the "Megalithic religion." There is general agreement that the original center of Megalithic culture was in Spain and North Africa; from there Megalithic waves carried it as far as India and Polynesia. This dissemination across three continents would, according to Huth, explain the enormously wide circulation of tales. Unfortunately, the new hypothesis is all the less convincing from the fact that we know next to nothing of the protohistorical "Megalithic religion."

Professor de Vries passes rather quickly over the explications put forward by the psychologists, though he dwells on Jung's contributions (pp. 34 f.). He accepts the Jungian concept of the archetype as a structure of the collective unconscious; but he rightly points out that the tale is not an immediate and spontaneous creation of the unconscious (as dream is, for example); it is primarily a "literary form," like the novel and the play. The psychologist neglects the history of folklore motifs and the evolution of popular literary themes; he tends to work with abstract schemas. These criticisms are justified—provided we do not forget that the depth psychologist uses his own scale and that, of course, "the scale creates the phenomenon." All that a folklorist can bring against a psychologist is that the latter's results do not solve *his* problem; their only value for him is in suggesting new approaches.

The second part of the book is devoted to Jan de Vries's own views. A series of well-conducted analyses (pp. 84 f.) show that the explanation for the sagas (the Argonauts, Siegfried) does not lie in tales but in myths. The problem of the poem of Siegfried is not to discover how it came out of scraps of legend and folklore "motifs" but how a fabulous biography could arise from a historical prototype. The author most aptly points out that a saga is not the conglomerate from a dust of "motifs"; the hero's life is a whole, from his birth to his tragic death (p. 125). The heroic epic does not belong to the popular tradition; it is a poetic form created in aristocratic circles. Its universe is an ideal world, set in an Age of Gold, like the world of the Gods. The saga is close to myth, the tale is not. It is often hard to decide whether a saga is narrating the heroicized life of a historical figure or, on the contrary, a secularized myth. To be sure, the same archetypes

—that is, the same exemplary figures and situations—appear alike in myths, sagas, and tales. But while the hero of the sagas ends tragically, the tale always has a happy ending (p. 156).

The author also dwells on another difference, which he considers primary, between the tale and the saga. The latter still assumes the mythical world, the former breaks away from it (p. 175). In the saga the hero is placed in a world governed by the Gods and fate. In contrast, the protagonist in folk tales appears to be emancipated from the Gods; his protectors and companions suffice to bring him victory. This almost ironic detachment from the world of the Gods is accompanied by a total absence of the problematical. In the tales the world is simple and clear. But, Jan de Vries remarks, life is neither simple nor clear—and he asks at what historical moment existence was not yet felt to be a catastrophe. He thinks of the Homeric world, of that age when man was already beginning to break away from the traditional Gods, without yet seeking refuge in the Mystery religions. It is in such a world—or, in other civilizations, in a similar spiritual situation—that Professor de Vries is inclined to see the auspicious soil for the birth of tales (p. 174). The tale, too, is an expression of aristocratic existence, and, as such, is close to the saga. But their directions diverge: the tale breaks away from the divine and mythical universe and "falls" to the level of the people as soon as the aristocracy becomes aware of existence as problem and tragedy (p. 178).

An adequate discussion of all these questions would lead us too far. Several of the conclusions reached by Jan de Vries must be accepted: the common structure shared by myth, saga, and tale, for example; the contrast between the pessimism of the sagas and the optimism of the tales; the progressive desacralization of the mythical world. As to the problem of the "origin" of folk tales, it is too complex to enter upon here. The chief difficulty lies in the ambiguity of the terms "origin" and "birth" themselves. For the folklorist, the "birth" of a tale is identical with the appearance of a piece of oral literature. It is a historical fact, to be studied as such. Hence the specialists in oral literatures are justified in disregarding the "prehistory" of their documents.

They are in possession of oral "texts," just as their colleagues the historians of literatures are in possession of written texts. They study and compare them, trace back their dissemination and their reciprocal influence, more or less as literary historians do. Their hermeneutics seeks to understand and present the spiritual universe of tales and is little concerned with its mythical antecedents.

For the ethnologist and the historian of religions, on the contrary, the "birth" of a tale as an autonomous literary text is a secondary problem. To begin with, on the level of "primitive" cultures the distance between myths and tales is less marked than in the cultures in which there is an immense gulf between the "lettered" class and the "people" (as was the case in the ancient Near East, in Greece, in the European Middle Ages). Myths are often blended with tales (and it is nearly always in this condition that ethnologists record them), or again, what has the prestige of myth in one tribe will be merely a tale in the neighboring tribe. But the concern of the ethnologist and the historian of religions is man's behavior toward the sacred as that behavior appears from the whole mass of oral texts. Now, it is not always true that the tale shows a "desacralization" of the mythical world. It would be more correct to speak of a camouflage of mythical motifs and characters; instead of "desacralization," it would be better to say "rank-loss of the sacred." For, as Jan de Vries has very well shown, there is no solution of continuity between the scenarios of myths, sagas, and folk tales. Moreover, if the Gods no longer appear under their real names in the tales, their outlines can still be distinguished in the figures of the hero's protectors, enemies, and companions. They are camouflaged—or, if you will, "fallen"—but they continue to perform their function.

The coexistence, the contemporaneity of myths and tales in traditional societies raises a question that, though difficult, is not insoluble. One may think of the societies of the medieval West, in which the genuine mystics are swamped in the mass of simple believers and even rub shoulders with certain Christians in whom alienation from the faith had gone so far that their participation in Christianity was purely external. A religion is always lived—or accepted and undergone—in several tonalities; but between these different planes of experience there are equivalence and homologation. The equivalence persists even after the "banalization" of the religious experience, after the (apparent) desacralization of the world. (To convince oneself of this it is enough to analyze the valuations of "Nature" by laymen and scientists after Rousseau and the Enlightenment.) But today religious behavior and the structures of the sacred—divine figures, exemplary acts, etc.—are found again at the deepest levels of the psyche, in the "unconscious," on the planes of dream and imagination.

This raises a further problem, which concerns neither the folklorist nor the ethnologist, but which preoccupies the historian of religions and will eventually interest the philosopher and, perhaps, the literary critic, for it also touches, even if indirectly, upon the "birth of literature." Though in the West the tale has long since become a literature of diversion (for children and peasants) or of escape (for city dwellers), it still presents the structure of an infinitely serious and responsible adventure, for in the last analysis it is reducible to an initiatory scenario: again and again we find initiatory ordeals (battles with the monster, apparently insurmountable obstacles, riddles to be solved, impossible tasks, etc.), the descent to Hades or the ascent to Heaven (or—what amounts to the same thing—death and resurrection), marrying the princess. It is true, as Jan de Vries has very rightly stressed, that the tale always comes to a happy conclusion. But its content proper refers to a terrifyingly serious reality: initiation, that is, passing, by way of a symbolic death and resurrection, from ignorance and immaturity to the spiritual age of the adult. The difficulty is to determine when the tale began its career of pure fairy tale emptied of all initiatory responsibility. It is not impossible, at least for certain cultures, that this happened at the moment when the ideology and traditional rites of initiation were falling into disuse and it became safe to "tell" what had earlier demanded the utmost secrecy. But it is not at all sure that this process was general. In a number of primitive cultures, in which initiation rites are still living, stories of initiatory structure are told and have long been told.

We could almost say that the tale repeats, on another plane

and by other means, the exemplary initiation scenario. The tale takes up and continues "initiation" on the level of the imaginary. If it represents an amusement or an escape, it does so only for the banalized consciousness, and particularly for that of modern man; in the deep psyche initiation scenarios preserve their seriousness and continue to transmit their message, to produce mutations. All unwittingly, and indeed believing that he is merely amusing himself or escaping, the man of the modern societies still benefits from the imaginary initiation supplied by tales. That being so, one may wonder if the fairy tale did not very early become an "easy doublet" for the initiation myth and rites, if it did not have the role of re-creating the "initiatory ordeals" on the plane of imagination and dream. This point of view will surprise only those who regard initiation as a type of behavior peculiar to the man of the traditional societies. Today we are beginning to realize that what is called "initiation" coexists with the human condition, that every existence is made up of an unbroken series of "ordeals," "deaths," and "resurrections," whatever be the terms that modern language uses to express these originally religious experiences.

Appendix II.

Basic Bibliography

We cannot here undertake to present and discuss the various modern interpretations of myth; the problem is of the utmost interest and deserves a whole book to itself. For the history of the "rediscovery" of myth in the twentieth century constitutes a chapter in the history of modern thought. A critical review of all the interpretations, from antiquity to our day, will be found in Jan de Vries's rich and illuminating book, *Forschungsgeschichte der Mythologie* (Verlag Karl Alber, Freiburg/Munich, 1961). Cf. also E. Buess, *Geschichte des mythischen Erkennens* (Munich, 1953).

For the various methodological approaches—from the "astral school" to the most recent ethnological interpretations of myth—cf. the bibliographies in our *Patterns in Comparative Religion,* pp. 435 ff. Cf. also J. Henninger, "Le Mythe en Ethnologie" (*Dictionnaire de la Bible,* Supplement VI, cols. 225 f.) ; Josef L. Seifert, *Sinndeutung des Mythos* (Munich, 1954).

An analysis of current theories of myth will be found in J. Melville and Frances S. Herskowitz, "A Cross-Cultural Approach to Myth" (in: *Dahomean Narrative,* Evanston, 1958, pp. 81–122). On the relations between myths and rituals, cf. Clyde Kluckhohn, "Myths and Rituals: A General Theory" (*Harvard Theological Review,* XXXV, 1942, pp. 45–79) ; S. H. Hooke, "Myth and Ritual: Past and Present" (in: *Myth, Ritual and Kingship,* edited by S. H. Hooke, Oxford, 1958, pp. 1–21) ; Stanley Edgar Hyman, "The Ritual View of Myth and the Mythic" (in: *Myth. A Symposium,* edited by Thomas A. Sebeok, Philadelphia, 1955, pp. 84–94).

For a structuralist interpretation of myth, cf. Claude Lévi-Strauss, "The Structural Study of Myth" (in: *Myth. A Symposium,* pp. 50–66).

A critical study of some recent theories, written from the point of view of "storicismo assoluto," in Ernesto de Martino, "Mito, scienze religiose e civiltà moderna" (*Nuovi Argomenti,* No. 37, March-April 1959, pp. 4–48).

Several articles on myth will be found in issues 4–6 of the review *Studium Generale,* VIII, 1955. Cf. especially W. F. Otto, "Der Mythos" (pp. 263–268); Karl Kerényi, "Gedanken über die Zeitmässigkeit einer Darstellung der griechischen Mythologie" (pp. 268–272); Hildebrecht Hommel, "Mythos und Logos" (pp. 310–316); K. Goldammer, "Die Entmythologisierung des Mythus als Problemstellung der Mythologien" (pp. 378–393).

A study rich in new insights into the structure and function of myths in archaic societies has recently been published by H. Baumann, "Mythos in ethnologischer Sicht" (*Studium Generale,* XII, 1959, pp. 1–17, 583–597).

The volume *Myth and Mythmaking,* edited by Henry A. Murray (New York, 1960), contains seventeen articles on various aspects of myth, the relations between myth and folklore, myths and literature, etc. Cf. also Joseph Campbell, *The Masks of God: Primitive Mythology* (New York, 1959).

Theodor H. Gaster offers a redefinition of myth in his essay "Myth and Story" (*Numen,* I, 1954, pp. 184–212).

The transition from mythical thought to rational thought has recently been studied by Georges Gusdorf, *Mythe et métaphysique* (Paris, 1953). Cf. also *Il Problema della demitizzazione* (Rome, 1961) and *Demitizzazione e Immagine* (1962), published under the editorship of Enrico Castelli.

World Perspectives

What This Series Means

It is the thesis of *World Perspectives* that man is in the process of developing a new consciousness which, in spite of his apparent spiritual and moral captivity, can eventually lift the human race above and beyond the fear, ignorance, and isolation which beset it today. It is to this nascent consciousness, to this concept of man born out of a universe perceived through a fresh vision of reality, that *World Perspectives* is dedicated.

Only those spiritual and intellectual leaders of our epoch who have a paternity in this extension of man's horizons are invited to participate in this Series: those who are aware of the truth that beyond the divisiveness among men there exists a primordial unitive power since we are all bound together by a common humanity more fundamental than any unity of dogma; those who recognize that the centrifugal force which has scattered and atomized mankind must be replaced by an integrating structure and process capable of bestowing meaning and purpose on existence; those who realize that science itself, when not inhibited by the limitations of its own methodology, when chastened and humbled, commits man to an indeterminate range of yet undreamed consequences that may flow from it.

This Series endeavors to point to a reality of which scientific theory has revealed only one aspect. It is the commitment to this reality that lends universal intent to a scientist's most original and solitary thought. By acknowledging this frankly we shall restore science to the great family of human aspirations by which men hope to fulfill themselves in the world community as thinking and sentient beings. For our problem is to discover a principle of differentiation and yet relationship lucid enough to justify and to purify scientific, philosophic and all other knowledge, both discursive and intuitive, by accepting their interdependence. This is the crisis in consciousness made articulate through the crisis in science. This is the new awakening.

Each volume presents the thought and belief of its author and points to the way in which religion, philosophy, art, science, economics, politics and history may constitute that form of human activity which takes the fullest and most precise account of variousness, possibility, complexity and difficulty. Thus *World Perspectives* endeavors to define that ecumenical power of the mind and heart which enables man through his mysterious greatness to re-create his life.

This Series is committed to a re-examination of all those sides of human endeavor which the specialist was taught to believe he could safely leave aside. It interprets present and past events impinging on human life in our growing World Age and envisages what man may yet attain when summoned by an unbending inner necessity to the quest of what is most exalted in him. Its purpose is to offer new vistas in terms of world and human development while refusing to betray the intimate correlation between universality and individuality, dynamics and form, freedom and destiny. Each author deals with the increasing realization that spirit and nature are not separate and apart; that intuition and reason must regain their importance as the means of perceiving and fusing inner being with outer reality.

World Perspectives endeavors to show that the conception of wholeness, unity, organism is a higher and more concrete conception than that of matter and energy. Thus an enlarged meaning of life, of biology, not as it is revealed in the test tube of the laboratory but as it is experienced within the organism of life itself, is attempted in this Series. For the principle of life consists in the tension which connects spirit with the realm of matter. The element of life is dominant in the very texture of nature, thus rendering life, biology, a trans-empirical science. The laws of life have their origin beyond their mere physical manifestations and compel us to consider their spiritual source. In fact, the widening of the conceptual framework has not only served to restore order within the respective branches of knowledge, but has also disclosed analogies in man's position regarding the analysis and synthesis of experience in apparently separated domains of knowledge suggesting the possibility of an ever more embracing objective description of the meaning of life.

Knowledge, it is shown in these books, no longer consists in a manipulation of man and nature as opposite forces, nor in the reduction of data to mere statistical order, but is a means of liberating mankind from the destructive power of fear, pointing the way toward the goal of the rehabilitation of the human will and the rebirth of faith and confidence in the human person. The works published also endeavor to reveal that the cry for patterns, systems and authorities is growing less insistent as the desire grows stronger in both East and West for the recovery of a dignity, integrity and self-realization which are the inalienable rights of man who may now guide change by means of conscious purpose in the light of rational experience.

Other vital questions explored relate to problems of international understanding as well as to problems dealing with prejudice and the resultant tensions and antagonisms. The growing perception and responsibility of our World Age point to the new reality that the individual person and the collective person supplement and integrate each other; that the thrall of totalitarianism of both left and right has been shaken in the universal desire to recapture the authority of truth and human totality. Mankind can finally place its trust not in a proletarian authoritarianism, not in a secularized humanism, both of which have betrayed the spiritual property right of history, but in a sacramental brotherhood and in the unity of knowledge. This new consciousness has created a widening of human horizons beyond every parochialism, and a revolution in human thought comparable to the basic assumption, among the ancient Greeks, of the sovereignty of reason; corresponding to the great effulgence of the moral conscience articulated by the Hebrew prophets; analogous to the fundamental assertions of Christianity; or to the beginning of a new scientific era, the era of the science of dynamics, the experimental foundations of which were laid by Galileo in the Renaissance.

An important effort of this Series is to re-examine the contradictory meanings and applications which are given today to such terms as democracy, freedom, justice, love, peace, brotherhood and God. The purpose of such inquiries is to clear the way for the foundation of a genuine *world* history not in terms of nation or race or culture but in terms of man in relation to God, to himself, his fellow man and the universe, that reach beyond immediate self-interest. For the meaning of the World Age consists in respecting man's hopes and dreams which lead to a deeper understanding of the basic values of all peoples.

World Perspectives is planned to gain insight into the meaning of man, who not only is determined by history but who also determines history. History is to be understood as concerned not only with the life of man on this planet but as including also such cosmic influences as interpenetrate our human world. This generation is discovering that history does not conform to the social optimism of modern civilization and that the organization of human communities and the establishment of freedom and peace are not only intellectual achievements but spiritual and moral achievements as well, demanding a cherishing of the wholeness of human personality, the "unmediated wholeness of feeling and thought," and constituting a never-ending challenge to man, emerging from the abyss of meaninglessness and suffering, to be renewed and replenished in the totality of his life.

Justice itself, which has been "in a state of pilgrimage and crucifixion" and now is being slowly liberated from the grip of social and political demonologies in the East as well as in the West, begins to question its own premises. The modern revolutionary movements which have challenged the sacred institutions of society by protecting social injustice in the name of social justice are examined and re-evaluated.

In the light of this, we have no choice but to admit that the *un*freedom against which freedom is measured must be retained with it, namely, that the aspect of truth out of which the night view appears to emerge, the darkness of our time, is as little abandonable as is man's subjective advance. Thus the two sources of man's consciousness are inseparable, not as dead but as living and complementary, an aspect of that "principle of complementarity" through which Niels Bohr has sought to unite the quantum and the wave, both of which constitute the very fabric of life's radiant energy.

There is in mankind today a counterforce to the sterility and danger of a quantitative, anonymous mass culture, a new, if sometimes imperceptible, spiritual sense of convergence toward world unity on the basis of the sacredness of each human person and respect for the plurality of cultures. There is a growing awareness that equality may not be evaluated in mere numerical terms but is proportionate and analogical in its reality. For when equality is equated with interchangeability, individuality is negated and the human person extinguished.

We stand at the brink of an age of a world in which human life presses forward to actualize new forms. The false separation of man and nature, of time and space, of freedom and security, is acknowledged and we are faced with a new vision of man in his organic unity and of history offering a richness and diversity of quality and majesty of scope hitherto unprecedented. In relating the accumulated wisdom of man's spirit to the new reality of the World Age, in articulating its thought and belief, *World Perspectives* seeks to encourage a renaissance of hope in society and of pride in man's decision as to what his destiny will be.

World Perspectives is committed to the recognition that all great changes are preceded by a vigorous intellectual re-evaluation and reorganization. Our authors are aware that the sin of *hubris* may be avoided by showing that the creative process itself is not a free activity if by free we mean arbitrary, or unrelated to cosmic law. For the creative process in the human mind, the developmental process in organic nature and the basic laws of the inorganic realm may be but varied expressions of a universal formative process. Thus *World Perspectives* hopes to show that although the present apocalyptic period is one of exceptional tensions, there is also at work an exceptional movement toward a compensating unity which refuses to violate the ultimate moral power at work in the universe, that very power upon which all human effort must at last depend. In this way we may come to understand that there exists an inherent independence of spiritual and mental growth which though conditioned by circumstances is never determined by circumstances. In this way the great plethora of human knowledge may be correlated with an insight into the nature of human nature by being attuned to the wide and deep range of human thought and human experience.

In spite of the infinite obligation of men and in spite of their finite power, in spite of the intransigence of nationalisms, and in spite of the homelessness of moral passions rendered ineffectual by the scientific outlook, beneath the apparent turmoil and upheaval of the present, and out of the transformations of this dynamic period with the unfolding of a world consciousness, the purpose of *World Perspectives* is to help quicken the "unshaken heart of well-rounded truth" and interpret the significant elements of the World Age now taking shape out of the core of that undimmed continuity of the creative process which restores man to mankind while deepening and enhancing his communion with the universe.

Ruth Nanda Anshen

New York, 1963

DATE DUE

DEC 1 9 1993		
DEC 3 1 1993		
JAN 0 2 1997		
OCT 08		
DEC 2 0		